Praise for "The Feminine ToolKit"

"It's an easy read that leaves you with a 'can-do' attitude toward do-it-yourself projects."
--*Lisa Marie Janeiro, SPFX makeup artist, Toronto, Ontario, Canada*

"Ohhhh. So that's what they're called and you can use them for that! There is nothing sexier than a woman who knows her tools."
--*Nerine Shaw, Mississauga, Ontario, Canada*

"Linda's abundant use of tips, real-life stories and plain simple logic, makes this book required reading for ALL women. You tell it like it is, with a refreshing twist of humour that keeps you wanting more!"
--*Christina Perreault, Toronto, Ontario, Canada*

"I love the descriptions, illustrations, and helpful tips. For someone who's never been very familiar with tools or with making repairs, I feel much more confident walking into a hardware store. The projects are well explained and achievable. I can hardly wait to get started!"
--*Malumir R. Beavis, writer, Toronto, Ontario, Canada*

"I wished I had this book when I first moved into my house, then I would have been "pretty" handy with tools. The Feminine Tool Kit will make you laugh, but it's full of practical ideas on how to do the simplest things in home repair. Bravo Linda, awesome!"
--*Urmelia Martin, Toronto, Ontario, Canada*

"Finally, a real 'How-to' book that can turn any Betty Crocker into Tim the tool 'WO-man' Taylor. Linda has a real knack for explaining things! With all the diagrams, tips, and 'by the way' notes, this easy-to-follow and understand book should be on every woman's bookshelf. Linda takes away the anxiety of learning & doing something new, and replaces it with knowledge and confidence in your own abilities. Very empowering. Being the 'handy-woman' of my house, and having just moved into a turn of the century home, this book is definitely going to be useful to me. I just might let my husband read it too!"
--*Angie Castelli, Toronto, Ontario, Canada*

The Feminine ToolKit

Every Woman's Guide to Tools and Home Repairs

Written by Linda Mentze
Illustrations by Mark P. Tjan

SynergySalad

Orangeville, Ontario, Canada

© Linda Mentze 2006
Illustrations © Mark P. Tjan 2006

Published by SynergySalad
75 First Street, Suite 227
Orangeville, Ontario L9W 5B6 Canada

Printed in the United States of America
First Edition

Library and Archives Canada Cataloguing in Publication
Mentze, Linda, 1956-
    The feminine toolkit : every woman's guide to tools and repairs / written by Linda Mentze ; illustrations by Mark P. Tjan.
Includes index.
ISBN 0-9738914-1-6
    1. Repairing--Amateurs' manuals. 2. Dwellings--Maintenance and repair--Amateurs' manuals. 3. Do-it-yourself work. 4. Tools.
I. Title.
TH4817.3.M45 2006   643'.7082   C2006-906703-1

SynergySalad products are available at special quantity discounts to use for sales promotion, employee premiums, or educational purposes. Enquiries please email **SynergySalad** at Sales@SynergySalad.com or visit our web site for more information at **www.SynergySalad.com**

SynergySalad is the trading name of PublishingSalad Inc.

I couldn't have done it alone

If I listed everyone that made a difference in my life, it would be another book. But there are some people who influenced me the most to write this book:

Mom – for encouraging me to explore the world

Grandma Rosa – for showing me early on that a single woman can survive and thrive

Tork – for teaching me the deeper meaning of values like integrity, honesty, and loyalty. And for supporting this project from the very beginning

Nerine – for inspiring me to write down the stuff I know

And most of all, my two best friends:

Urmelia, a quiet inspiration and source of peace in my life. She has been a confidante and a treasure in my life for 20 years, constantly challenging me to be a better me for others.

Brian, a very special friend for 20 years. Through his friendship and rather warped sense of humour, I realized there are people in this world that I can love unconditionally and that can love me unconditionally.

And ultimately, **God** has played the most important, yet silent, part in all this. He gave me the desire to help others, and He has given me this outlet to share that desire.

Contents

Introduction
Why Tools? Why You?

Introduction .. Why Tools? Why You?

When we were kids, our dads had tools in the basement or garage, and our parents did all the repairs around the house. Later on, it was our brothers, our boyfriends, or even our brother's friends that fixed things that needed repairs. In those days, people didn't replace something just because it happened to be a little broken or needed some TLC.

But we were never asked to help with these repairs. Except one summer I remember having the "honour" of carrying my Dad's toolbox and handing him tools as he tried to install a small bathroom in our basement. I got dirty and several times had water spray in my face when a copper fitting didn't (fit, I mean).

And if something went wrong with my 2-wheeler (for you younger gals, we didn't have 10-speeds or mountain bikes back then; a 3-speed was greeted with "wow, great bike!") my Dad or younger brother were the only people that Mom would let work on it.

Years later, when I lived on my own and wondered why I never learned how to fix things, I realized that none of my girlfriends knew how to handle tools, either. We all heard our family say things like: "Tools aren't lady-like." "Nice girls don't get their hands dirty." "Let your brother do that, he's much more mechanical than you."

And most of us believed these things. We told ourselves that someone else would handle it for us, that we really didn't have the aptitude for tools or repairs, that we were into more creative things like music or whatever, that we didn't like tools or doing things that could wreck a manicure. Or worse, have guys think we were tomboys.

Well, I'm here to tell you that we were all sold a bogus story, and some of us are still paying the bill. I look at it this way – if a guy can do it, a woman can too. We're organized, we read instructions, and we pay attention to details. So what's the problem?

Education.

Pure and simple, we don't know how to do these things because no one taught us.

Like anything else, if a woman wants to learn something she can, it's a matter of finding someone to teach her.

My story

I learned everything that I talk about in this book first-hand. The hard way - by doing things and then learning how not to do them. By trying things and seeing what happened. By asking friends how to do something, then doing it myself. Some of the things in this book were simply the result of experimentation, and some ideas I got from a home-improvement shows.

I ended up doing these things for myself because I chose to remain single. The boyfriends I've had over the years (serious and casual) were mostly incapable of doing home repairs. There was one time I had a leaky kitchen faucet – just a simple job to replace the washer, but Mr. Handyman flooded my kitchen (and ruined the wallpaper with the spray). We didn't last long as a couple – that wasn't the only thing he couldn't do right. Nuff said…

My grandmother and my mother couldn't do home repairs either, and they owned nothing more masculine than a small screwdriver to fix the handles on their pots.

My grandmother divorced my grandfather in 1955 and never remarried, so she had to fend for herself. And my mother couldn't count on my dad to do things around the house - he was fine with mowing the lawn or fixing the back stairs, but he wasn't good at anything complicated (see the story above about the basement bathroom).

Both Mom and Grandma became liberated before it was an actual social movement. They both taught me – through their actions and their example - that I was capable of doing anything. I was smart enough and creative enough to figure things out.

Just like you.

But probably the most valuable lesson I learned – believe it or not, from a macho boyfriend many years ago – was that I could do anything if I wanted to and was willing to learn how. He taught me how to work on my car (I replaced the radiator, and replaced the "idiot" engine lights with gauges), and once I realized that most simple things to repair really are simple, the world was a bigger, more exciting place.

For those of you old enough to remember the 1980's, I **loved** the MacGyver TV show. Not just because I thought Richard Dean Anderson was (and still is) adorable, but I was fascinated by the way he was able to take small ordinary items and turn them into something useful.

Now, not everyone needs to be able to make a microwave oven out of a paper clip and a rubber band, but the idea of making creative objects out of simple things stuck with me.

Many of the things I've made or fixed were the result of just thinking outside the box. For this reason, when I go through a home-improvement store, I don't see what things on the shelves for what they are for – I ask "what I can make from that?". Anyone can learn to do this if they just look at the world from a slightly different (some would say weird) perspective.

Your story

So it's time to learn to do these little things for yourself. Whatever you might have been taught in the past, by well-meaning parents or condescending teachers or macho boyfriends, tools and home repairs are just part of life. They aren't outside your abilities, they aren't scary monsters that you need a man to protect you from (yes, I took grammar in school and did very well actually, but this is my book so I don't care if the sentence is structured correctly or not).

You should be able to:
- Change a fuse or a lightbulb, or put in a new light fixture (that dingy thing in your rented apartment kitchen is **so** out of date)
- Replace a toilet seat (my god, what are those stains anyway?)
- Paint your bathroom (who would choose black and turquoise for a bathroom?)
- Put up shelves without pulling out the plaster
- Assemble an "easy-to-assemble" bookcase, computer desk, or bar stool
- Re-pot plants before they break out of those green plastic things and take over the house like an alien from some 1950's sci-fi movie
- Create something unique out of stuff other people consider junk

4

Some of these I'll explain in this book. For some you're on your own –
think of these as your final exam for the "The Feminine ToolKit" course.

I realized some time ago that some things are made to appear
complicated or "only for professionals" because that's how the
professionals make their money. If everyone could do things on their
own, what would we need them for?

Now I have nothing against handymen or professionals (some are quite
cute), but they can be expensive. And those kinds of relationships just
lead to trouble anyway. Not really worth the cash or the heartache.

This book is to help you figure out the things you can do yourself, what
tools you should have around (just in case), some ideas for decorating on
a shoestring budget, plus a few tips along the way. But there will be
times you need to call in professional help.

Learn your own limitations – be willing to learn and to try, and also
know when to call in an expert.

Introduction .. Why Tools? Why You?

Chapter 1

Hand Me That Thingamajig, Please

Hand Me That Thingamajig, Please

No one is exactly sure when humans created the first tool. Until that fateful day, humans used whatever they found around them (sticks, twigs, stones) to manipulate their world. Monkeys and even some birds do this as well, using whatever is at hand to dig insects from inside a log for their dinner (yummy). The difference between these animals and humans is that we learned to not just use what was around us; we learned to **make** tools to suit our needs.

Stone Age humans made simple tools from the materials at hand – stone, wood, bone. The material and manufacturing methods have changed in the past 100,000 years, but the design and purpose are basically unchanged since the first human used a rock to shape an arrow head.

Besides weapons (knives, arrows, spears) the first tools were stone hammers and chisels. Even up to recent times, nails were used to connect wooden things together. It wasn't until the Industrial Revolution that metal screws, nuts and bolts started being used.

Along with the discovery and taming of fire, it was the making of specialized tools (axes, knives, spears, etc.) that enabled humans to control their environment more than any other creature.

So tools, especially hand tools, have a long and important history in the development of our civilization.

Now, you don't put on makeup with a paintbrush. You don't cook an omelette with a shovel. And you don't do home repairs with tweezers and rubber bands.

You need the right tools to do the job – this chapter is a guide to the hand tools you need.

Hand tools are those metal-and-wood things that hang on pegs in garages, the hardware department at The Home Depot®, Rona ®, or Sears ®, or on carpenters' belts. By the way, it's the weight of all those tools that makes their pants slide down and reveal that rear-end Grand Canyon you see when they bend over your sink and mutter something about "overtime".

They have macho-sounding names: wrench, hammer, ratchet, pliers, screwdriver, etc. And they all come in different types and sizes – I think the idea is to make the tool-consuming public believe that you need six hammers, eighteen screwdrivers, and thirty-two different wrenches just to assemble a tricycle or repair a lamp.

You don't need one of everything – in fact, unless you're apprenticing to repair the Space Shuttle you don't need more than just a few well-chosen tools to cover most basic home repairs.

Hammers

Used to pound something into something else (well, I couldn't think of a simpler description). They're useful to put a nail into a board or the wall. Yes, I know your shoe works fine in a pinch, but nails can make a mess of the heels on your shoe, and the sole just isn't thick or strong enough.

Tip:	To hammer a nail without hitting your finger, use a hairpin (bobby pin) to hold the nail while you hit it – slip the hair pin around the nail so the nail is at the bendy end of the hair pin. Sliding the nail into the teeth of a comb would also work, or twist a twisty-tie around the nail to give you a handle.

Claw Hammers

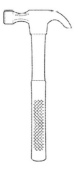

These have a two-fingered hook on one end, used to pull a nail out of a board or the wall. They can also be used to pry open a can of paint or open a can of coffee. The other end is the "business" end – the head that you use to hit a nail to drive it into the wall or into wood. Hammers come is all kinds of sizes and weights. Basically, the longer the handle, the more power you can bring to hit something, but the harder it is to actually hit what you're aiming at. And the heavier the head, the more power when you hit the nail. And the more damage you can do if you miss it and hit your thumb. Some hammers have wooden handles, but if you hit something really hard you could split the wood and then you have a piece of junk. Other hammers have steel handles that have rubber hand grips attached – they're a little

9

more expensive and a little heavier, but there's no chance of the head flying off and hitting the neighbour's cat.

Ball-peen Hammer

 I don't see much use for a heavy metal tools with a flat head on one end and a round metal ball on the other end – the only time I've seen this type of hammer is in old murder mysteries and "B" horror pictures. I'm sure someone uses them, but I have never had the need for this thing.

Mallet

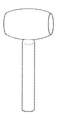 These are usually hard rubber, so you can pound on something without denting it. Good to put the lid back on a can of paint so it doesn't dry out (then you just wasted all that paint). It also makes a nice booming sound when you pound on your hardwood floors to get your downstairs neighbours to turn down their stereo. But other than that, you can probably go your whole life without one of these.

Screwdrivers

No, not vodka-and-orange juice. These are hand tools that are used to drive screws into or out of things, among other uses. I don't recommend you use a screwdriver to butter your bread or fiddle with a toaster.

There are 3 main 'styles' of screwdrivers, and they all come in lots of sizes. That's so you have to buy at least 2 or 3 sizes just to match all the different screws out there (you didn't think hardware stores are there to make it easy, do you?). And they all come in different handle and blade lengths – the longer the screwdriver the harder you can turn it and the stronger it is.

A lot of screwdrivers also have magnetized heads – just great for keeping the screw on the head while it's being driving into the wood.

10

Or for fishing any small metal object from the bathroom drain or from under the couch.

Tip	So you know which way to turn a screw (or a nut or bolt), remember the saying "Righty tighty, lefty loosy".

The colour of the screwdriver handle indicates the size of the head:
- green handle is a #1 driver, for No. 5, 6, and 7 screws
- red handle is a #2 driver, for No. 8, 9, and 10 screws
- black handle is a #3 driver, for No. 12 and larger screws

Flathead

It's not an insult - these are screwdrivers with a flat spatula-like head that fit into a slot on the head of a screw. They're also good for opening paint cans or prying things apart. But I don't like using them for screws, because the blade can slip out of the slot on the screw and really mess up the wood you're working on, or gouge a piece out of the wall or, worse yet, your hand. I do have a large one and a tiny one around – they are useful all-around tools to have.

Phillips

These are the ones that have a 4-pointed star head, to match up with screws with a cross-shaped slot in the head. Obviously invented by some guy named Mr. Phillips. I'm not fond of these – if a screw is in really tight, you can either strip the slots in the screw or wear down the head of the screwdriver (whichever is softer will wear out first). While I don't like them for screws, they can make interesting impressions on cookies before baking.

Robertson

These are the ones with a small square head, to match up with screws with a small square hole. These are my preferred screwdrivers. The head on the screwdriver can't strip the square hole on the screw very well, and they don't slip out easily. But since screws come with different-sized holes, you need two or 3 different-sized heads to fit all the different screws you might have.

Hex Key (also called Allen Wrench)

Technically, this isn't a screwdriver. But it is used to drive screws into things, so let's not get too technical. A hex key is one of those strange small L-shaped tools you get in a box of bookcase from Ikea. It's like a six-sided Robertson without a handle. Nice idea, but only good for Ikea furniture. Hard to find screws that work with it. But if you have a few around, hang onto them – never know when someone has an emergency bookcase to put together.

Wrenches and Pliers

These are the grab-and-twist tools. They hold things with one hand while you do stuff with the other hand (yeah, I know what that sounds like, but there you go).

Some terms to help you understand the types of joints wrenches and pliers have. These are usually part of the tool description:

Slip Joint   Have an adjustment in the middle so you can open them wide for large bolts or fittings.

Locking   Let you clamp onto something and lock the tool in place - they do the holding for you.

Groove-joint   Ones with adjustable joint positions to hold different sized items.

Long-nosed   What they sound like – they have long pointed noses instead of blunt ones - great for fixing jewellry and other small things.

Diagonal   Look like a clamshell to me – they look like they'd be good for cutting wire, but not holding things – the part that grips is sharp and could leave marks

Linesman   Serious, heavy-duty tools with big square heads for gripping large bolts or cutting heavy wire.

Torque Wrench (also called a Ratchet)

I think these are cool, and I even have a set that I never use. A thimble-like thing slips onto the end of a long handle at right angles, and you put the thimble over the bolt or nut you're trying to tighten or loosen. Then you crank the handle in one direction to tighten, swing back (this doesn't loosen what you've done so far) and crank again to tighten more. Car mechanics seem to love these (they aren't hard to use and they do work real well), and I've seen guys using these very gracefully. But you do need a collection of the thimble things for the different sizes bolts out there. If you do a lot of metal work or car repairs these are great. It's also good to have a set in your trunk – when the car mechanic sees them, they'll think you understand cars and may not over-charge you (buy an old set at a garage sale so they look like you know how to use them).

Monkey Wrench

This is the old plumbers' wrench you see in the movies and cartoons. They are sometimes called pipe wrenches. They are big heavy things (usually red) that have a little wheel on them that opens or closes the jaws. You clamp them on a pipe or fitting and twist them to loosen or tighten, but they can slip, so what you're working on should have flat sides to grip better – these don't work well on rounded objects. If you're big into doing your own plumbing work, then get yourself a good sized pipe wrench. But if you're not into plumbing, you really don't need one of these (unless you work in an airplane repair shop).

Adjustable Wrench

This is sort of like a pipe wrench, but a lot smaller, and they are usually chrome (well, bright silvery colour even if it's not real chrome). They're handy when you want to hold things in place while you work on them, or when you aren't strong enough to use pliers to keep the object steady.

13

Box Wrench

These dainty things are usually used for bikes, snowmobiles, cars, and lawnmowers. But they don't adjust, so you need a lot of different-sized ones for all the different-sized nuts and bolts you'll find on different items.

Pliers

These are tools like giant tweezers – you have to hold them closed to keep the grip. They're easy to use, but they can slip so be careful.

Needle-nosed Pliers

These are useful for smaller, delicate work. They're great for craft, jewellry making or repairs, and other small projects.

Wirecutters

These are like pliers, and are used to cut wire (like speaker wire or lamp wire). Most also have a slot where you can strip the plastic covering to expose the bare wire without cutting through the wire itself. I don't have to tell you - **only** do this if the appliance is **unplugged.** These are handy to have around if you are doing any wiring; they can also come in handy for other projects (you never know when you need to trim the outside of something without cutting through it completely).

Saws

These are tools to cut wood or other items – they're like really big steak knives or serrated bread knives. If you're doing a lot of wood work (e.g., building something from scratch), you may want to get a power saw such as a circular saw (see the chapter on power tools). But for small things such as cutting a shelf shorter, a hand saw is fine.

Hand saws

These are sometimes called "cross cut" saws, as the teeth in the blade alternate in direction. Most have wooden handles and steel blades, and are not expensive. These are good for cutting shelves or other wood items shorter. They don't cut very smooth – the cuts can be rough, and it's easy to cut a little wonky, so draw your cut line on your wood and go carefully. Also, they can make a mess of your hand or foot if you get them in the way – good idea to have the first aid kit handy.

Hack saws

These are all metal, and the teeth on the blade are very small and close together. Usually used to cut metal (like aluminum strips or pipes), they make neat cuts but are harder to work with – they take a lot of elbow grease. They can work on wood, but it takes a lot of time and effort. And most cuts made in metal require sanding off the burrs (the little stubble left on the edges). But hack saws are useful to have around if you need to cut something a little denser than wood. The blades are thin and can break, but are easy to replace (make sure you buy the right length replacement blades).

Pipe cutters

These are nifty little tools for cutting metal pipes or tubing (like copper tubing for wind chimes or water fountains). The idea is you put the tool on the pipe and tighten it down. Then turn the tool around the pipe and a wheel scores the pipe. Then you tighten the tool a little more and go around again. Continue until the pipe is cut through. These make nice smooth cuts in pipes and are easy to use. They come is all kinds of sizes from the very small to the very large – each one cuts a range of pipe diameters.

By the way I made a wind chime out of copper tubing normally used for sink plumbing, and I use a pipe cutter to cut the tubing - it comes in 2m (6 ft) lengths. Copper tubing comes in different diameters, from 5cm (2") to about .32cm (1/8"). The sound a wind chime creates is related to a number of things:
- the shorter the tube, the higher-pitched the sound
- the wider the diameter, the lower-pitched the sound
- the thicker the tube material, the more mellow the tone
So I cut 5 different lengths of tubing, drilled 2 small holes at the top across from each other, and string fishing line through the holes and attached them around the outside of a circular piece of wood. I then hung another tube in the middle, that I had wedged into a wooden ring so the wood would strike the 5 hanging tubes in the wind. It worked fine, but if you're going to do this, be careful about the length of the tubes – you can't just cut random lengths and have it sound harmonious. There's a relationship between tube length and the musical note it makes.

Hand Tools for special (aka weird) stuff

Awl
To make holes in things like leather or vinyl. A sharp nail or the tines of a fork will work just as well.

File
Like a giant nailfile, it's used to smooth edges of metal items.

Level

This is a useful item, especially if you want to hang shelves or pictures straight. It's a sealed tube almost completely filled with water, so it has a small bubble of air. When you put in on a flat surface like a shelf, the bubble shows you whether you're

completely horizontal. You don't need a huge one - they can be as long as a meter (40").
One that is 15-20 cm (6" – 8") is probably long enough for most situations. You can also get laser levels that shine a beam of horizontal light you can use as a guide for pictures or shelves or whatever. Nice idea, but the inexpensive water levels work fine.

Staple Gun

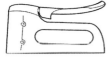

A must-have if you are re-covering chair bottoms or barstool seats – these are like office staplers, but the staples you get are stronger than the ones for paper, and the best staple guns are the ones where you press down on the front of the gun to fire the staple. Some nice-looking staple guns have an older design where you push down on the back of the gun to fire the staple, but it can get tiring very quickly when you use these ones a lot.

Scraper/putty knife

This is a flat blade that can be anywhere from 2cm to 15cm (1" to 6") wide on a handle – like a spatula. It's used to spread joint compound or crack filler on walls (though in a pinch they're great for spreading mayo on sandwiches – just make sure it's clean).

Utility Knife

These come in all kinds of styles and brands. Basically they are a handle to hold a single-edged razor blade to cut carpet, tile, trim wallpaper, etc. You can buy replacement blades for the model you get, but check that your replacement blades are meant to fit the handle. The style and size is up to you – I prefer the one that looks like a silver pencil – they're smaller and not as strong, but are easier to work with for small projects.

Clamps

These are mechanical things that hold items together while you work on them, or while glue dries. Nice and all, but not usually necessary (but if you have a couple around they could come in handy).

My Hand Tool Recommendations

Hammers
- Get an all-steel claw hammer, 240 - 375 gm (8-12 oz.) weight, 28-30 cm (11-12") long, with a rubber-covered handle. It's not too light and not too heavy – good for most around-the-home use.

Screwdrivers
- Two flat head drivers – one 27-30cm (11-12") long, and one 7-9cm (3-4") long
- One Phillips – a size 2 red handle, 20cm (8") long should be good
- Two Robertsons – a size 1 green handle, 20cm (8") long, and a size 2 red handle 20cm (8") long
- Handle length is really up to you – but choose drivers that fit nicely in your hand (not too fat or too skinny) but long enough so you aren't trying to hold them with just a couple of fingers
- You might also consider a set of mini-screwdrivers for tight spots (but don't go cheap, the small heads can wear down very quickly)

Pliers
- One mid-sized slip joint pair 20cm (8") long
- One small needle-nosed 14cm (6") long
- One wirecutter with wire stripper slots

Wrenches
- One 25cm (10") long adjustable wrench, one 13-14cm (5-6") long locking wrench
- Get a torque wrench set if you're going to be doing any car repairs
- For the best size for your hand, try them on if you can (like shoes). And get ones with a built in wire-cutter if you can

Saws

- One hand saw, 30cm (12") blade
- One hacksaw, 20cm (8") blade – also pick up some replacement blades, they're thin and can break fairly easily
- Two pipe cutters, one .32-.64cm (1/8" to 1/4") outside pipe diameter, and one .64-5cm (1/4" to 2") outside pipe diameter

Others

- A staple gun if you'll be recovering a chair seat or bench. Get one that works when you push down at the front of the tool, instead of the back. You'll also need staples to fit the one you buy.
- A scraper is a great all-around tool – I have a 2.5cm (1") wide one and a 9cm (4") wide one. I'm not sure when or why I bought either – maybe I was just in a shopping "zone" one day and picked them up.
- A utility knife is so versatile it's hard to list everything.

By the way	If you go camping or cabin-weekending, consider getting an axe. I don't mean a little hatchet the size of a hammer with a chopping blade instead of a nail-hitting head. No, I mean a full-sized axe. The one I bought when a friend and I went camping in northern Ontario one summer was a beauty – 76cm (30") long handle, with a 1.3kg (3-pound) head. Keep the axe sharp (a sharpening stone is the best way to sharpen the blade) as a dull axe could bounce off the log and cause injury. You should also have a small hatchet as well, for trimming branches off small logs for the fire.

Hand Me That Thingamajig, Please

Chapter 2

Power To the People

Power to the People

Power tools actually did exist (sort of) centuries before the invention of electricity. They were powered by steam or water or animals, but were not in common use in the home or small shops. Water-wheels powered the milling of grain, steam powered printing presses and a few other industries, and horses or other large animals powered farm activities.

With the Industrial Revolution in the mid-1700's, consistent, reliable, and affordable power for factories and industry became an important goal, beginning with Benjamin Franklin's experiment with a kite one stormy night in Philadelphia in 1747. In 1879, Thomas A. Edison not only perfected the electric light bulb, but is also responsible for the development of generating plants and methods of delivering electric power to homes and factories – the first utility company (the General Electric Company) was born in 1892.

Small electrically-powered tools and appliances for household consumers didn't become wide-spread until after World War II. Technology and inventions during the war had peace-time applications that were quickly marketed by manufacturer's to the reasonably affluent middle class. And with the start of the Baby Boom in 1948, the demand for time-saving devices of all kinds exploded.

And as society changed into more urban, white-collar employment, there was more leisure time for people. With leisure time, for some reason, comes the desire to build something, preferably out of wood or metal. So the home workshop and hundreds of different power tools evolved in garages and basements all over the world.

Now, electric or battery-powered tools aren't necessarily critical, but they can make home repairs or building things easier. Instead of putting together a bookcase or computer desk just using your own muscle power, the right power tool can make it go faster with less fatigue. And believe me, girls, there is something satisfying about powering a screw into a shelf or wall in a couple of seconds. It's a lot like the feeling on a motorcycle – something masculine but still feminine about all that power. We're not supposed to feel it – it's supposed to be directly related to testosterone. But even the most delicate female has some of that male hormone in her blood (whether she admits it or not).

So you may not need or even want a garage or basement full of electric power tools - they take up a lot of room, and you really do need a fairly good-sized workbench to use them.

But a small select collection of the most useful and versatile machines are like luggage – good to have around when you need them, as long as it doesn't clutter up the closet too much. But if you don't want to spend money on these tools right away, you can rent them as you need them from your local hardware or do-it-yourself store. That way you can get the tool for the job without committing to a particular one. Kind of like test-driving a car before you buy one.

Most brands make their power tools in both corded and cordless models. Corded are great if you have a lot of heavy work to do (like building an entire kitchen).

Cordless are convenient, go-anywhere items. They can be a little heavier (that battery pack isn't just a couple of AA batteries), but that's more than compensated by the convenience. And if you get a couple of different tools from the same manufacturer, you can get them so that the battery pack is interchangeable between the tools. In which case, have 2 battery packs – one in the tool and one charging as backup.

Rotary Tools

These gadgets are not necessary – they're really only useful if you are doing some fancy wood carving or other serious crafts. They're like those fancy nail-care kits our mothers had in the 80's with all the attachments to buff and manicure nails. They come with small sanding bits, wood-carving tools, and lots of other neat attachments. But they aren't very powerful – they're intended more for fine, delicate work (like crafts, wood-carving, etc.). There are different brands out there, but the bits from one brand usually fit the other brands.

Hand Sanders

Sanders can be very useful if you want to sand off the paint or finish on a large wooden item, or if you want to round off sharp edges of any wooden item such as a box, bookcase, or shelves. Not very good for calluses on your knees or heels; too much power and if you aren't careful you'll have a lot of blood to clean up. They're also useful for sanding stains off countertops (don't overdo it, tile doesn't grow back).

There are 2 basic types - palm sanders (which are square and noisy) or sanders/polishers (which are more delicate and a little quieter). The latter usually have sanding pads that are pear-shaped or triangle-shaped which are easier for getting into corners.

Power Drills

You could go with a cordless drill. No cords to worry about, right? Sounds convenient, right? Well, yes, and no. Cordless drills don't have the same power if you are working on heavy or thick wood. And depending on the model and the battery, you may have to recharge the battery if you are doing a lot of stuff all at one time. Not to mention that the cordless drills can be a little heavy – that battery pack is hefty. But cordless drills are convenient for tight spaces, or places where you don't have an outlet.

I used to use hand screwdrivers to repair or build things. Maybe I've gotten smarter, or maybe just lazier. A power drill with a screwdriver bit will do in 10 seconds what it might take a minute or 2 to do by hand.

For example, a few years ago I bought a put-it-together-yourself bookcase (5 feet tall and 3 feet wide). It came with all the hardware and screws needed to put it together, and they even pre-drilled the holes so it was easy to assemble. But cranking on the screws by hand got tiring very quickly. So the next time I bought a do-it-yourself piece of furniture (my Ikea computer desk), I had already bought a power drill. It took maybe a quarter the time to put together than it would have by hand.

You don't have to get an expensive drill – watch for sales at whatever store you prefer for power tools and pick them up at a deal before you actually need them.

Some terminology you need to know:

Amps   The power of a tool – the larger the number, the more powerful the tool (like horsepower on a car). More power means it will go faster, and the more power it will have for a stubborn screw or tough wood.

Bits   These are small pieces that fit into a collar on the drill that do the actual work. You can get bits that will drill holes (different bit sizes to drill different-sized holes) as well as bits that are like screwdriver heads for driving screws in and out of wood or the wall. Both drill bits and screwdriver bits are useful, so consider getting a "set" that includes a bunch of both types.

Chuck   The way you change the drill bits or screwdriver bits – keyless chuck means you can change bits with just your hands, key chuck means you need a small tool to loosen the collar that holds the bits in the tool. The collar of the chuck that actually holds the bit is tightened in the same direction   as   the drill spins, so that as you use it the chuck won't loosen on you (a great design idea).

Having had basic power drills (one speed only), I realized quickly that variable speed drills are more convenient. Variable speed means just that – you can go as slow or as fast as you need, so you don't overscrew anything because you're going too fast.

Glue Guns

These are fabulous little items – they heat glue "sticks" to the melting point that you use to glue small items onto other things (like handbags, shoeboxes, etc. – see the chapter on Craft Projects). They're also great for gluing a loose edge of a decorative strip on a purse, or the trim on the edge of a chair, stool, or table

There are two types, and you need to get the right kind of glue stick for the type of gun you have.

High Temp   As the name implies, they get fairly hot and can burn your skin quite badly if you touch the hot tip of the glue gun, or get a drop of melted glue on you. The glue is fairly strong, so it's good for heavy items or things that will get a lot of wear.

Low Temp   These don't get as hot as the high temp, but the glue isn't as strong either – not good for heavy items or things that have a lot of wear. But they're great for light craft projects

Other Power Tools

There are other power tools – reciprocating saws, jigsaws, circular saws, bench grinders – serious hardware. But unless you're building a house or cottage from scratch, these aren't necessary. If you find you need something serious, rent from a do-it-yourself store.

By the way	I thought a jigsaw would be a great tool to cut down some wood shelves. Nope – bad idea. Jigsaws may work fine on those home improvement shows, but I found it jumped and skittered about so much that the final result was a crooked and messy cut edge – basically ruined the shelf (I used it anyway but it's in a corner so I don't see the cut edge). So if you want to cut down shelves, take them to your local hardware or do-it-yourself store, or use a hand saw. It may be more work, but you'll get a nice clean cut and your bookcase will actually be straight (the one I built with those shelves is – well, let's call it "abstract" and leave it at that, okay)?

My Power Tool Recommendations

Drill

- A cordless drill, reversible is important, variable speed is nice. Get one that has a storage case for the drill and the bits – makes it easier to use if you aren't digging through your junk drawer for a part you need.
- Drill bits – don't go cheap. Cheap bits will bend or break if you put too much pressure on them, so they can be a waste of money. You can get drill bit sets that come in a case from 5 pieces to over 200 pieces. You don't need the big set – look for a set that includes drill bits and screwdriver heads in one case. Go for ones that are meant for wood or metal – those with a titanium coating makes it go a little smoother.

Sander

- If you are doing any work with wood (like bookcases, tables, shelves, or whatever) you may want one of these. They aren't that expensive and don't take up a lot of room. Find one that comes in its own case for storage.
- I have one that has the face pad in the shape of a triangle (sort of) - it's great for getting into corners and small places. Its rather noisy, but it does vibrate nicely and feels good when I work with it.

Glue Gun

- If you're doing any decorative or crafty projects, this is a must-have (along with the right glue-sticks). You can get mini-glue guns (that use glue sticks that are about as thick as pencils) and they work fine.
- I prefer the high-temp mini-glue gun.

Power to the People

Chapter 3
Care and Feeding of Your Tools

Storing your Tools

If you have a good-sized area in a basement or garage, you could build a storage area and workbench for your tools. But a lot of us live in smaller homes or apartments, so we don't have the luxury of major storage space.

You have several options for tool storage, depending on the amount of space and how many tools you have.

I live in a cozy apartment in downtown Toronto, so I have ample room for me and my stuff. But tools aren't something I want taking up space in my living room or kitchen, so I had to come up with something that keeps my tools and all the little widgets like screws and bolts tidy and accessible.

I bought one of those metal tool cabinets with drawers (the one I have is about 15" high and 15" wide, with about 12 different-sized drawers.

Most of the drawers are just the right size for holding screws, nuts and bolts, nails, and other small things. There is also one large drawer that holds my screwdrivers and pliers.

This unit is in my linen closet, and I hang my hammer and saws on hooks on the inside wall.

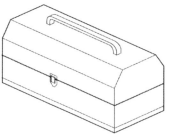

Another option is a toolbox. They come in metal or plastic, and most have a tray on top for small things and room under the tray for the hand tools. You've seen them used as tackle boxes for fishing, and in the 1980's I knew a few girls that used them as makeup cases.

Or check out the newer tool pouches – like a backpack or large tote bag, they're usually nylon or canvas and hold a lot of stuff. These are very useful, because they aren't as heavy as a tool box. And since they're soft they won't cause damage to your tools. But they hold a lot so they can get heavy, and even though they have a lot of pockets and compartments things can get a little lost in the bag.

For my power tools, I keep them in the boxes they came in; a couple I bought that came with a plastic storage case that holds the tool and the accessory pieces (like drill bits or sandpaper). I store these outside on my balcony – my linen closet is small and I keep other stuff in there that I need more often (towels, extra bathroom tissue, sheets, etc.)

If you have the room, consider getting a larger tool cabinet that can either mount on the wall or sit on a workbench or table.

Or a microwave cart or cabinet with doors would store most tools fairly neatly as well if you have the room (even a corner of the kitchen will do if you have the space).

If you don't have a lot of space in your rooms but you have a good-sized closet somewhere, you can put a small cabinet or cart in the closet – keeps your tools out of sight but still accessible.

Tool Safety

Tools can be dangerous if not treated with care and respect. Think "safety first" when working with tools:

- Wear protective glasses or goggles whenever you use power tools, or when you are working overhead, chiseling, sanding, or scraping anything, especially if you wear contact lenses
- Wear ear protectors if you use power tools - some are loud enough to damage your hearing if you don't wear ear protection
- Keep your hair tied back, and make sure you don't have loose clothing that can get caught in a power tool. Use a bandana or hair band as well if your bangs aren't long enough to be tied back
- If you're sanding, sawing, or using spray paint wear one of those filter masks – they may look dumb but it's better than inhaling the fumes or dust
- If you have a tool with a cracked handle, replace it – don't take a chance on it breaking while you're using it
- Keep a first aid kit on hand just in case of a minor slip or cut
- For all power tools, read the owner's manual and know how to use it correctly
- Keep all power and hand tools out of reach of small children
- Unplug all power tools when you change settings or attachments

Treat your tools with care – keep them clean and lubricated, keep them out of the weather, and if possible hang up the tools that have cutting edges so they don't nick or dull each other.

Use WD-40® to lubricate saws, and a light machine oil or 3-IN-ONE® Oil for power tools (as indicated in the owners manual or instructions for the tool)

WD-40 and 3-IN-ONE are registered trademarks of the WD-40 Company

Extension Cords

If you're using power tools, I recommend you get one of those big red or yellow round extensions cords. These are rated for outside use, so they are water-resistant and are meant for a lot of electricity.

Ordinary household extension cords aren't heavy enough to use with a power drill or circular saw. But ordinary extension cords are fine if you're using a rotary tool or glue gun.

Just be sure that the cord is in good condition – no nicks or tears in the plastic covering, no scorching or burnt areas around the plugs. If in doubt, throw it away and get a new one – it's not worth the few bucks a new cord costs to take a chance with fire or electrocution.

And if you have to plug it in somewhere far from where you're working, use duct tape to tape it down to the floor to reduce the risk of tripping on it.

Chapter 4

Bits and Pieces, Nuts and Bolts

It's inevitable.

At some time, you're going to need a screw or a nail or a hook or a washer or some other little piece of metal to make something or fix something.

It's also inevitable that all the screws and nails and hooks and washers and other little pieces of metal that you have hanging around the house won't be the right size or the right type.

But you can be somewhat prepared by having a small but diverse assortment of those little bits and pieces on hand.

Screws

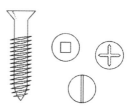

These little marvels of man's ingenuity come in hundreds of styles, thousands of sizes, and millions of uses (well, maybe not millions, but a heck of a lot just the same).

They are little pointy pieces of metal with threads on them to grip the wood or whatever you're screwing (keep it clean, now).

Their main purpose is to attach two things together. If you're dealing with wood, it's usually a good idea to drill a "pilot hole" in the wood pieces that is just slightly narrower than the screw you're using, so that the wood doesn't split when you attach the pieces.

The threads on the screw are what bite into the wood and hold it all together (it's the friction between the wood and the screw that actually does the holding – just thought I'd toss a little science in for fun).

The two main materials where screws are used are wood and metal. And if you go down the "Screws and Bolts" aisle of a hardware store, you'll see them arranged by "screws for wood" and "screws for metal".

So you need some of each.

The length of the screw you need for any particular situation is dictated by the thickness of whatever you're screwing together.

For example, if you are screwing a shelf end-on to a bookcase upright, and the upright is 1 cm (1/2 ") thick the screw has to be at least that long just to get through the upright. Then you need at least that much length again to screw into the shelf. If it's going to hold books or heavy items, the screw should go into the shelf at least 3 times the thickness of the upright.

But if you're screwing a shelf bracket to the underside of a shelf, you don't want the screw coming out the top of the shelf, so the screw has to be shorter than the thickness of the shelf.

The head of the screw fits a particular screwdriver (you remember the section on these). And the size of the head "slot" determines the size of the screwdriver you need.

Screws are packaged with a couple of different numbers that can get confusing.

The first number – e.g., #6 – refers to the diameter of the screw. The larger the number, the thicker the screw.

The next numbers are the diameter and length (usually in inches even in Canada).

Bolts

These are like screws, but without a pointy end. They connect things by putting the bolt through holes in the things you want to connect, and putting the nut (like a tiny metal donut with threads on the inside) on the end to keep it all tight. They come in all sizes and styles as well, just like screws. You need a wrench of some kind to tighten them. I usually use 2 wrenches – one to hold the bolt and one to tighten the nut (those metal nuts can ruin a good manicure).

I have a small collection (well, collection is a rather fancy term for a bunch in a jar) and the only problem I have is that I can never find a nut to fit the diameter of the bolt I want to use.

So if you buy them, get the packages that have both the bolts and the nuts together.

Washers

These are like even thinner metal donuts without threads. They're basically spacers – you can use them on a screw that's too long to make it shorter (well, sort of – try it and you'll see what I mean). They're also good if the screw head is small and the material you're screwing into is soft or delicate – the washer distributes the pressure from the screw head over a larger area.

They're useful to have around – I bought one of those little clear plastic boxes (they look like makeup cases for mice) that have about a hundred washers in different sizes so I didn't have to pick and choose.

Hooks

For hanging pictures, for hanging decorations, for hanging coats, for hanging whatever, you need hooks. You can get ones that glue onto the wall, but they make a mess when you pull them off.

Or you can get ones that screw into the wall, but then you have a hole to patch if you want to move it.

Or you can get these nifty little hook sets that you nail into the wall – they do make a hole, but it's tidy and smaller than the hole a screw would make.

And they can hold quite a bit of weight. You can also buy those little clear plastic boxes with all kinds of picture hooks and picture wire in them if you have a lot of pictures or mirrors to hang up.

Other things you should have around

Duct tape   Useful for a lot of things (Canadians know about duct tape) – stronger than masking tape and easier to work with than packing tape.

Glue   Epoxy glue (the kind to repair china) is useful for light gluing of a lot of small things like jewellry, upholstery, metal items, etc. Wood glue is good for...yes, you guessed it – gluing wood together. Goop® is a good all-around glue for heavier items.

You can find all kinds of different glues (in tubes, tins, and bottles) in home improvement and hardware stores. My advice is to read the packaging and pick the right product for what you want to do.

Nails   Assorted small ones for tacking down carpeting or nailing small items, and some larger ones for nailing boards (I sometimes use the larger ones to put a small hole in wood to give me a good start to drilling a pilot hole – keeps the drill bit from skipping around while it's drilling).

Twine   To tie things up or tie things down (I love the English language, it can be so creative).

Sandpaper   You never know when you need to sand something smooth. Steel wool is also useful to have around.

Dust masks   If you do any sanding, spray painting, or stripping wood, you need these to keep the dust and fumes out. Some products are toxic and should not be inhaled. And wood dust makes a mess of your nostrils if you breathe it in.

Safety Glasses   Anytime you use a power tool or chemical products, you should wear safety glasses. No project is worth losing an eye over.   Get ones that fit comfortably and have side vents to keep things cool.

Lubricant   No, not what you're thinking. I mean a product such as WD-40® or 3-IN-ONE ® oil to use on squeaky hinges, rusted bolts, or to lubricate and protect your tools. They work well on sliding doors that don't slide well, windows that don't open or close easily, or anything metal or wood that sticks. Not for plastic items – for these, use a touch of Vaseline® or baby oil (not more than a smidgen).

Measuring Tape   The best for home repairs is one of the metal measuring tapes that retracts into the little case. Metal measuring tapes won't stretch or warp like the fabric ones for sewing will, so they are more accurate over time. You may also want to get a solid metal ruler up to 1 m (40") long for marking straight lines on wood for cutting, etc.

WD-40 and 3-IN-ONE are registered trademarks of the WD-40 Company

Chapter 5

Painting Isn't Just For Artists Anymore

This chapter is all about putting paint on things – like walls, furniture, shoes. Or putting wallpaper on things – like walls, furniture, shoes (we'll go into the shoes a little later).

Types of Paint

Primer

This is like a base coat of polish on your nails – it fills in tiny cracks and gives the wall a surface that is meant for the paint to stick to it well. Read the directions on the can, but a rule of thumb is oil primer under oil paint, latex primer under latex paint. Don't mix them up – you can if you want, but be prepared for a mess.

Latex

This water-based paint dries quickly and doesn't have much smell, so it's great for small rooms or apartments. Brushes or rollers can be cleaned with soap and water, so you can reuse your tools. It's not usually easy to clean if it gets dirty (like fingerprints or cooking grease) and it can peel or discolor if it gets wet a lot, so it's not that good for kitchens or bathrooms. For bathrooms and kitchens, go for one of the new "anti-mildew" paints – you'll be glad in the long run.

Oil-based

Takes several hours to a day to dry completely, and has an odor that some people may find hard to take (it tends to give me a headache if I'm around it too long). Only use when you have good ventilation. Good for bathrooms and kitchens - waterproof once it's dry and is easy to wipe off stains and marks. You need turpentine or mineral spirits to clean up (from your hands, from the floor if you spill it, from your tools) and that also smells pretty bad. It's also called **alkyd** paint.

Tip:	If you're using paint that has a strong smell, add a capful of vanilla extract to the paint. It won't affect the paint, but will cut the smell.

Spray paint

Like it sounds, paint in a spray can. You usually need turpentine to clean up (though you can use nail polish remover to get it off your hands). It can be expensive, because there isn't a lot in a can and if you have a large piece to paint it could take several cans to cover it completely. But it's handy for painting things with crevices or curves like a light fixture or wicker table.

If you're going to use spray paint, wear one of those white paper dust masks. Not just because the fumes can be toxic and not because of the smell (which I don't like, but I have a friend that loves that kind of smell). No, it's a simple suggestion – if you breathe in the spray you'll end up with coloured hairs inside your nose (yes, I know "gross!"). A lesson I learned the hard way – just passing it on (and I tried using nail polish remover on a cotton pad to get rid of the paint – don't try that). Also wear latex gloves (the kind you use for hair colouring) to keep the stuff out from under your nails.

Tips:	If you have an unusual situation like old wallpaper you can't get off, or severely damaged walls, talk to an expert at a hardware or home improvement store. You could strip the wallpaper off, or do what I did – paint over the wallpaper with an oil primer first (oil primer because if you use latex you could end up turning the wallpaper into oatmeal mush on your wall), then paint the final finish in oil paint. But don't skip the primer – if you just paint over the wallpaper, you'll spend an entertaining evening watching the paper roll off the wall.
	If you're painting a large area like a room or 2, or if you are moving a lot of things around as you paint, consider doing it au naturel (for those of us that only know English, it means no clothes). No laundry afterwards, and it's a lot cooler if you're painting in the summer.

Paint Finishes

Flat   No shine when dry (like it's been dusted with baby powder). It hides tiny flaws in the surface since it doesn't reflect light.

Satin   A little gleam to the finish, like buffed nails. Not shiny but not flat either.

Gloss   Like clear polished nails, it's a shiny finish – this one shows flaws on the surface more because of the way it reflects light.

Sealers

These are used to give a clear finish to your painted items – especially ones that will have wear and tear on them, or where the paint finish is delicate or could be damaged by water or use.

You don't need a sealer coat on most wall surfaces, but it won't hurt if you do put one on. Just remember that if you want to paint that wall in the future, you'll need to remove the sealer layer or the new paint won't stick.

Sealers come in finishes just like paint, and also come in types (latex or oil-based). Choose the type that goes with the type of paint you used. You can also get clear varnish or sealers in spray cans – easy to use when the item is complicated or textured.

Paint Prep

Whatever you're painting, you need to prepare the surface so that your final result doesn't fall off, peel, or roll away.

Small nail holes or cracks in a wall can be filled with a product called "filler", or "joint compound", or "patch filler". You're best off to get the kind that is "non-shrinking" – no point filling in a crack only to have the crack show up again because the filler shrank when it dried.

It's hard to name it without using a specific brand. But if you go to the guy at the paint counter and tell him you want to fill small holes or tiny cracks, he'll show you the right stuff to get. It usually comes in a tube like toothpaste.

By the way	I tried a trick a 'friend' of mine taught me when I was moving out of my first apartment in Vancouver – he suggested I just use toothpaste to fill in the holes. No one would notice. Well, they will notice if you use a coloured toothpaste. And it's just bad form to do that to someone moving in after you – toothpaste will dry up and fall out of the holes, and it won't hold a nail either.

Use a scraper or putty knife (or a spatula if you don't have one) to push the filler into the hole or crack and smooth the edges (your finger will work fine, but wash the stuff off quickly as it's tough to get off once it dries). When the compound is dry (usually a few hours or even overnight), sand the surface smooth with a sanding block or sandpaper before painting.

Wallpaper should be completely stripped off the wall before painting (if you can).

Some wallpaper is called "dry strippable" which is supposed to mean that it's easy to peel off the wall. Well, maybe in the first week after it was hung. But I've found that most times, when you peel it off you just peel off the upper printed layer, and the paper backing with the glue stays on the wall.

You can rent steam machines that are like big flat irons that steam the glue in the paper to loosen it – but you have to score the wallpaper with a tool called a scorer that is a wheel with little barbs on it to put tiny holes in the wallpaper surface so the steam can get through.

Or you can use a chemical stripper solution that you spray on the walls (again, works better if you score the wallpaper first). This is messy but works well – a lot of gluey goopy stuff to clean up afterwards, but generally a good clean surface when it's done. If you have allergies or asthma, don't use the chemical method.

Furniture Paint

Paint for furniture comes in the same kinds of paint as you use for walls. In fact, if you prepare the furniture correctly, you can use ordinary wall paint to paint a dresser, bookcase, or table.

But be careful if what you're painting already has a finish or paint on it. If that's the case (like an old end table you find at a yard sale that has nice lines but horrid yellow paint on it), you need to strip it down to the bare wood first.

And you just might find something really beautiful when all that paint comes off, and may decide just to put on a clear varnish to protect it (like clear nailpolish to add shine and protection).

If you don't strip off the old stuff, at least rough up the finish with sandpaper or a sanding tool so that the new paint has something to stick to (they call it "giving the surface teeth"). But be prepared to have your new paint peel off if you scratch the surface anyway.

If you do want to strip the paint completely, you have a couple of options.

There are chemical paint strippers that work very well – but do it outside, the fumes are unhealthy.

Residue from stripping paint is both toxic and highly flammable. Dispose of it in a responsible manner. Put residue and all used rags and paper towels in a metal covered container outside, as those materials can catch fire on their own (spontaneous combustion). Read the directions on the package.

If the paint isn't too thick, consider simple sanding. You might also try steel wool pads soaked with mineral spirits to work the paint off – this can be smelly, messy, sweaty work, but a great way to get some stress out of your system.

You may need several coats of paint to get the finish right – if so, lightly sand between coats (the paint has to be **dry** or you'll make a mess of it) and wipe the dust off with a slightly damp rag or a tack cloth (this is a piece of cloth that is sticky and holds the dust when you wipe).

Check out the chapter on "Refinishing Wood Things" for some more information.

Craft Paint

This comes in small bottles that you can get at home improvement and craft stores. There isn't usually a lot in one bottle (2 oz or 60 ml) but it's usually enough for small craft projects. It comes in hundreds of colours, plus you can mix colours together to make your own shade. But if you do mix your own shade, make enough for your entire project – you'll never get exactly the same shade if you need to mix up another batch. Store unused mixed shades in a plastic bottle with screw top (like a travel bottle).

Some come in metallic finishes which is nice for adding a fake (faux) gold leaf to items that have a texture or pattern to the surface, like picture frames or carving on wood furniture. For this effect, use a dry brush dipped in the metallic paint, then wipe most of the paint off onto a paper towel. Then gently brush over the raised part of the surface – if you put on too much use a damp cloth to wipe it off before it dries.

Craft paint is fine for painting just about anything. Since it's inexpensive and comes in small bottles, you can have lots of different colours around for different things.

By the way   I used craft paint to paint fake tiles on my kitchen backsplash – I used a sponge cut into a 3" square, and dipped it into a mix of green, sage, and white craft paints to stamp the "tile" decoration on the wall over the main base colour. Not perfect like real tiles would be, but very inexpensive. And easy to change when I get tired of it – I can just paint right over it and I have a blank slate to do something else.

Painting Tools

To put paint on a wall or furniture, you need a brush or a roller. Or both.

Brushes

Depending on the paint you're using, you need different bristles in your brushes.

There are 3 basic brush types

Natural bristles	Use with alkyd or oil-based paints
Synthetic bristles	use with latex paints
Foam	can be used with any paint. Not expensive but they don't last long; fine for quick touch-ups only.

The larger the brush, the wider the paint application at one time. But there comes a time when the brush is too wide to handle well, or when it's larger than the area you are working on.

For craft projects, you may want some small artist brushes (they're like makeup brushes or the ones we used in art class in school). They're small so they're easy to control and good for small or delicate work, but not much good for large items.

Rollers

You need a roller handle, roller cover, and roller tray. I suggest you also get a threaded broom handle to screw onto the end of the roller handle, to make it easier to reach high spots. Rollers can apply paint more quickly than brushes, and the coverage is usually fairly even.

Rollers come in nap sizes – the length of the fibres on the roller cover. A good rule of thumb is: the smoother the surface you're painting, the shorter the nap of the roller. And the larger the nap, the more paint you'll use just to coat the roller.

Drywall, wallboard, smooth plaster, wood	.32-.64cm (1/8" to 1/4")
Light-textured stucco, concrete, or rough wood	.64-1.27cm (1/4" to 1/2")
Heavy-textured surfaces, concrete block, or brick	1.9-2.5cm (3/4" to 1")

Sponge Rollers

These are usually smaller rollers (they need a different handle) and are useful if you are painting a piece of furniture with a lot of flat surfaces like a dresser or bookcase. They can leave a nice smooth surface – great if you are using a gloss latex paint (you don't want any brush marks or roller "dimples" on a glossy finish).

Roller trays

Get a good metal tray, then buy the cheap plastic liner trays to go inside. The metal keeps the tray from bending or tilting, and the liner means cleanup is simply "toss the liner out".

Paint Pads

These are useful to apply paint along baseboards, door jambs, corners, or at the wall-ceiling junction. You can use most paint pads with either latex or oil paint.

But be careful you don't go too light with the paint – these paint pads tend to leave less paint on the wall than a roller or brush so you could end up with an uneven coat if you try to save paint.

Painting Techniques

You can use these techniques on a wall, furniture, or basically anything you want to paint.

Except the car, that should be painted by professionals. No matter how well the paint matches your car colour, it just doesn't work. I've even tried nailpolish – I mean that's enamel like car paint, and it dries shiny, right? Wrong – tried that when I scratched my boyfriend's red Buick, and boy did he let me have it. I thought it looked fine, but that's when I learned that you don't mess with a man's car. Ever.

Anyway, these techniques usually work best when you use latex or craft paints.

For anything new you try, experiment on a small board or piece of plain paper first, to get the hang of it and see if what you have in mind is what you'll like when it's done.

Sponging

1. Paint the surface with your main "base" colour and let it dry.
2. Take a sponge and dampen with water (wring out any excess)
3. Dip the sponge into another colour, then blot the excess paint onto a paper towel
4. Dab the sponge over the first colour, changing the angle and filling in where you want this second colour
5. Do this as many times as you like, using different colours - be sure to rinse out the sponge very well between colours. If you leave the paint wet when you go to the next colour, the colours will blend a little and you'll get an interesting effect. Or you can let each colour dry before going to the next one.
6. When it's completely dry (overnight is best, just in case), paint a clear varnish or sealer over the entire item and let dry at least another 24 hours before using it.
7. Rinse the sponge thoroughly when you're done, then let it air-dry completely before you put it away.

Ragging

Like sponging, you use something to put a second layer of paint on the base layer.

Crumple up an old rag (one without lint) and you can either:
1. Use the rag to put a second paint on your dry base colour
2. Paint an entire coat of your second colour over your dry base colour, then use the rag to take off some of the second layer. Work fast, latex paint dries very quickly.

Decorative roller

You can buy rollers in home improvement and paint stores that have a patterned texture on them, so they leave a pattern when you paint. These are fine if you want to create a subtle colour variation, but if you use a bright or bold colour with these rollers the effect is rather garish and (in my opinion) tacky.

Stamping

This is like the old "potato stamp" art we did as kids. Take a household kitchen sponge and cut it into a shape such as a star, abstract, or a 10cm (4") square – the square lets you create the look of tile using paint instead of the mess and expense of actually installing tile.

Fake Tiles

Paint your base coat and let it dry. Then dip your stamp into the next colour paint and carefully place on the wall and evenly press down on the entire stamp. Lift off carefully and continue. When you're finished, let it dry completely then seal with a clear topcoat sealer. Tiles are usually square, so your sponge stamp should be square as well. But to get a weathered look, tear tiny pieces off the edges so the paint won't be perfectly straight – it will look aged because the edges will be ragged.

My Paint Recommendations

Paint

- Unless you're painting something that will be around moisture, go with the latex paint. I prefer the satin finish (I think it's just a little classier than the flat finish without the garish look of the gloss).

Brushes, rollers, roller trays, etc.

For small craft painting:

- Get three or four small craft brushes (they're like long-handled eyeshadow brushes). You can get these anywhere crayons or kids paints are sold

For wall/furniture painting:

- One 5-8cm (2-3") wide brush - get the right bristles for your paint
- One roller handle - a good metal one so it will last a long time
- Roller covers: depending on the kind of painting you're doing - check the nap on the roller cover for the right height
- Roller tray: get a metal one, then some cheap plastic liners - they're only like a buck or so and you can throw them away after your project.

Sponge painting

- Cheap kitchen sponges (the large ones) are fine for sponge painting.
- You may also want to get a good-sized sea sponge – the texture it gives sponge painting is very natural and organic and they last a long time if you take care of them.

Other stuff

Painters tape is a great item to have around. It lets you tape off areas you don't want painted, then when the paint is completely dry you can carefully peel away the tape and you have a nice clean line and no cleanup to worry about.

Chapter 6
Paper on the Wall

So you've decided to wallpaper the bathroom or the hallway. Good for you. Wallpaper can create a warm, interesting wall or room if done well. But if done poorly, you should consider leaving town before the landlord sees it.

Wallpaper can be used on almost anything. You can find wallpaper made of burlap, cork, embossed paper, fabric, foamed vinyl, foils, grasses, hand or screen prints, and washable prints.

It's sold in what are called double-rolls, and most come pre-pasted – this means you don't have to put the paste on it yourself – very neat. But pre-pasted wallpaper has to soak in water to activate the paste. They even make a special cardboard tray just for this (what will they think of next?).

Patterns on wallpaper repeat – so what you see in the wallpaper book will repeat over and over again (the roll will tell you the repeat measurement). A pattern that repeats every 15cm (6") or less will look busy. Larger patterns with a repeat of 30cm (12") or more will look more subtle and peaceful, especially in a small room.

The wallpaper you put up today could be around for years - think "years" when picking out your pattern or colour. Your taste will change over time, so be sure you love the paper before you start.

If you have holes or cracks in the walls, the paper will shrink into them when it dries and your wall will look like a dart board, so fill those holes!

How much paper do you need?

You don't want to get caught short (no, not a comment on the vertically-challenged). When you wallpaper, there will be waste. You need to match the pattern, you'll need to cut around windows and doors (don't cover them up – I saw that once on "I Love Lucy" and while it was hysterical it was a little silly).

The more distance between repeats, the more paper you'll need to match patterns, so the more waste you'll have the more rolls you'll need. So get an extra roll or two, in the same dye lot (dye lot is the tone and intensity of the colours, and if you get different dye lots your wall will look very weird).

To figure out how many rolls you need, measure the height and width of each wall, then multiply them to get your square area.

Subtract 1 square meter (10 square feet) for every door or full-sized window. Add together the areas of each wall for a total wall area.

Wallpapering Basics

What you need
- Wallpaper
- Wallpaper tray
- Wallpaper smoothing tool (like a large Styrofoam comb with a soft fabric-like pad)
- Extremely sharp knife or blade for trimming edges
- Step ladder or stool to reach the high parts of the wall
- Kitchen sponge (a large one)
- Seam roller – a small rolling pin on a handle (you can get them in craft stores, hardware stores, or do-it-yourself stores) to make sure the seams are completely stuck
- Optional: a joint blade or putty knife at least 4" wide to use to hold the wallpaper in place when you trim it

How to do it
1. Prep the walls – remove any nails or hooks, patch any holes or cracks and let the patch material dry completely, then sand smooth
2. Put together the wallpaper tray and fill with water.
3. Measure the wall length for your first strip –start in a corner and work your way around the room. Cut the wallpaper about 15cm (6") longer than that measurement. Roll it up with the paste side out, and completely submerge it in the wallpaper tray water. Let

it soak for a minute, then pull it out using the metal rod to keep the roll in the water as you pull it out (you'll see what I mean when you do it).

4. Leaving about 8cm (3") overhang at the ceiling and 2.5cm (1") overhanging the adjacent wall, put the top of the wallpaper at the top of the wall in your starting area, making sure the strip is hanging straight. Use the smoothing tool to smooth the paper down, working from the centre out to get rid of any air bubbles. Wipe the strip with a damp sponge to remove any excess water and glue (rinse the sponge often as you work). The glue is real tough to get off once it's dry, and it doesn't look nice at all.

5. Trim the excess paper by holding the blade of the putty knife in the corner where the ceiling and wall meet. Use a single-edge razor to cut off the excess paper at the ceiling. Slide the putty knife along the wall as you cut the paper. Once the ceiling is trimmed, do the same to trim the excess paper at the floor. Clean off any excess glue that got on the base molding or the ceiling with a clean, damp sponge.

6. Use a seam roller (not a steam roller, a **seam** roller, like a tiny rolling pin sort of) to press the edge of the wallpaper down. This will ensure that the edge is securely stuck to the wall.

7. Repeat with the next strip and continue around the room.

Wallpaper borders are the same process, except they are usually in horizontal strips, not vertical ones like wallpaper.

| **By the way** | I once stripped the wallpaper off my bathroom wall, but I didn't take off the paper backing layer that was left behind. I didn't think about it, so I painted over it with a water-based (latex) base paint. Well, what happens when you put water onto paper – the paper becomes paste and makes a real mess. Well, I didn't feel like stripping it all off and sanding it all down, so (and I don't recommend this mind you) I let it all dry. Then I painted over it all with an oil-based primer and let it dry. Then I just painted over it with my final colour (latex) and voila! I had a finish that looks like Venetian plaster. Well, sort of. But it is a unique finish and I don't think I could have gotten the look if I had tried to make it happen deliberately. |

Chapter 7

Creativity is a State of Mind

This chapter is about doing things that other people might not even think of. Like painting your shoes, making your own purse or tote bag, creating decorative storage boxes, creating your own jewellry...

Painting things

Believe it or not, you can paint just about anything. As long as the surface doesn't have a finish on it already, you can paint it. And as long as the paint doesn't ruin the item (things like paper don't take water-based paints too well).

I have painted shoes – usually I use spray paint, but I use sandpaper to remove any shoe polish or other coating on the shoes. You can't paint shoes that are man-made materials (aka vinyl or plastic) but leather or canvas takes paint quite well if you prepare the surface.

For items with texture or a lot of crevasses or weaving (like shoes, handbags, wicker or rattan items, etc.), consider spray paint instead of paint you apply with a brush. Sure, the spray gets in the air, but it coats more evenly and quickly than trying to get a brush into all the little cracks.

By the way   Why do I paint shoes? A couple of reasons:
1. I find it hard to find styles I like that are comfortable. And once I find a pair I really like, often they don't come in the colors I want. So I buy them anyway and paint them the color I do want (white shoes are easier to paint than any other color).
2. Sometimes I get a pair of shoes I love and get them all broken in. But then I change my mind on the color, or they get dull or boring. So I paint them – sometimes the original color but usually something more fun.
   I find spray paint is the best for shoes – it usually lasts longer, goes on smoother, and I can get into every crack and seam easily.

Ways to Decorate Things

Whatever the item you're creating, you can decorate a number of ways. There are probably others I haven't listed here. Just take ordinary things around the house and let your imagination go wild.

Remember – there are no rules on this stuff. It's pure anarchy.

Paint As we've covered previously – anything can be painted if you prepare it well and just use a little imagination. Just be careful to make sure the item is prepared well.

Wallpaper If it's a box or other fairly simple item, cover in wallpaper just as you would a wall. Be careful to smooth out any wrinkles - unless you want that look which can be interesting when using abstract wallpaper. Check out what they call "roll ends" of wallpaper or discontinued patterns – you can get some interesting papers fairly cheaply (especially if you only need a small amount of paper).

Wrapping paper also works well, you just have to glue it down with white glue since it isn't pre-pasted

Tissue paper I have used tissue paper to decorate items – it can be a very interesting look. You can either leave the tissue paper smooth and glue it down, or you can try what I did. I crumpled the tissue paper up, then smoothed it flat and glued it down to the front of a dresser. Then I painted it once the glue was dry. The look was like crackled paint or a stucco-like texture. Best of all, it was pretty cheap. If you use a tissue paper that is already the colour you want, you don't have to paint it after the glue is dry. But you may want to paint on a clear varnish to protect the paper from moisture and dirt.

Fabric Use white glue (I like to water it down a little to make it easier to work with) to coat the object well, then smooth your fabric over it. Work out the wrinkles - again unless you want that rumpled look - then let dry. You can paint it after that if you want an additional effect. Or you can use one of the new spray adhesives on the market – they are easy to use, not very messy, and will stick fabric or paper fairly well. I've even done mosaic-type little boxes that had different fabric swatches glued on, kinda like a patchwork quilt.

Stuff

Glue small things of pretty much any kind to objects:
- seashells
- buttons
- candies
- uncooked pasta
- uncooked lentils or beans
- nuts in the shells (like brazil nuts, almonds, filberts – great for Thanksgiving or Christmas)
- pine cones
- beads
- the inside guts of an old clock or watch – very abstract, very retro
- small silk or dried flowers
- small bits of wood or small stones (these take good strong glue to keep them on)
- whatever you have around that you like

If you use delicate items, spray the entire piece with a clear varnish once the glue is completely dry to protect everything. It will also keep the colours from fading due to contact with the air.

Some Things to Create

Shoe boxes for decorative storage boxes

Since these are usually cardboard, they usually stand up better if you cover them with wallpaper or fabric instead of paint. The paint can 'melt' the paper of the cardboard and turn it into mush (water + paper = mush). But if you prime the box with Jesso (used to prime artists' canvases) or with an oil-based primer, or if you use oil-based paints, you can paint interesting and attractive storage boxes.

Select a box in good condition (no dents or tears) and paint the entire surface (inside and out, box and lid) with primer. Let it dry completely (overnight).

When it's dry, paint a solid colour or a pattern – whatever you like. Use stencils that you can get at any craft store to make pictures. If you are painting with several different colours, let each colour dry completely before going on to the next colour.

Plant pots

Clay pots especially are easy to paint and look great when grouped together. The pots should be completely clean (use a vegetable scrubber and warm soapy water) and completely dry (use an oven at around 200°F for an hour or so, or leave them in the sun for a day).

Prime the pots with a neutral primer paint, and let dry completely.

Then have fun painting your designs. Use stamps or brushes – you can use a leaf as a stamp by painting one side and stamping it onto the surface. Do the same with anything that has a reasonably flat surface to paint on – careful lifting it off the pot surface.

Handbags

Like painting shoes, it's better if there is no finish on it and if it's leather or fabric. Neutral canvas tote bags can be inexpensive to buy, but look great with your own look painted or glued on.

Clothing

You need a special fabric paint for items like t-shirts, scarves, etc. But you can paint pretty much any pattern or image you like.

Some paints state you need to iron the garment after the paint has dried to set it. Read the directions.

Creativity is a State of Mind

Picture frames

Strip off any old varnish or paint first, otherwise your new paint will peel off. Then paint, or glue items to the frame as discussed above.

Statue stand

I didn't know what else to call this – maybe "pedestal" is good. Basically, this is a tall narrow stand to display just one thing, like a statue, plant, or object d'art.

I took two 2X4 pine boards cut to 125cm (4 feet) long, glued them longways together with wood glue to make a reasonably close cube-shaped rod. Then I screwed a 30cm (12") round piece of flat wood to the bottom to make the base. After the glue dried completely, I sanded down all the corners and the seams where the wood joined (2X4's are not perfect, and they aren't quite 2" X 4" despite the name). I mixed some sawdust with the wood glue to fill in the seams so they were flush with the rest of the wood. I let that dry overnight and kept sanding. When it was smooth and I was happy with it, I painted the whole thing in white with gold and tan veining to look like marble.

I have a very special object sitting on top – it's a piece of driftwood redwood root that a woodcarver in Lindsay Ontario carved into an open vase for me.

Making a Tabletop Water Fountain

The trick to making one of these tabletop fountains is what do you want it to look like – what do you want it to be made out of?

You can make a tabletop fountain out of just about anything: natural rocks, clay pots, sculpted stone, seashells, crystal, wood...almost anything. Be creative – think outside the box of what you could buy in a store. Maybe you have a pair of shoes you'd like as a fountain – why not?

What you need

- A waterproof bowl or container
- A pump (you can get a fountain pump at home improvement stores or garden centres) with plastic hose
- Something to have the water flow over (rocks, wood, etc.)
- Water
- Optional: floral wire, fish tank gravel, glue gun and glue sticks

The size of all this is up to you. But the larger the fountain, the heavier it is and the more "stuff" you need to create the design. Plus the larger the bowl, and the bigger the pump you need.

You might try using some of that expanding foam-in-a-can they use to weatherproof and seal cracks around windows and door frames. You can spray it into a mounded shape around the clear water tube, and when it dries completely it's lightweight but also waterproof. It's a kind of yellow colour, so get the type you can paint (you'll need oil-based paint probably – read the instructions on the can of foam.

How to do it

1. Paint or decorate your container however you like, make sure you let any decorations dry completely, then completely cover with a waterproof (oil-based) clear sealer.

2. Test the pump's power before you put your fountain together.
3. Put the pump in the sink with the hose attached, and fill the sink with water until the entire pump is covered.
4. Plug the pump into an outlet and see how hard the water flows through the hose. They usually have a small knob or switch on the side of the pump that lets you control the flow of water.
5. Adjust until it's right for you.
6. Set the pump in the bottom of the container, with the electric power cord and hoses attached. You may want to test the power of the pump before you build anything, so it doesn't spray everywhere when it's finished.
7. A nice way to cover the pump, wire, and hoses is to use small stones or gravel (like the ones for fish tanks – they come in all kinds of colours and aren't expensive). Layer in your larger items - rocks, drift wood, lava rocks (the kind for gas barbecues are great), whatever you're using.
8. Work your hose around the back of the piece, using floral wire gently wound around the hose and the ends of the wire tucked into your piece to hold the hose in place.
9. Build up your piece as you want. Use a glue gun to glue the objects together and give the piece stability – be generous with the glue. Or use a waterproof glue you can get from any hardware or do-it-yourself store.
10. Some items such as rocks or broken clay pot pieces may fit together fine without needing any glue.
11. Don't use a glue gun to glue anything to the hose, you could melt it and then you have a leak and water everywhere.
12. Once you've built it up as far as you want, run the hose over the top. You may want to have something "cap" the hose to hide it. A flat rock with a little hollow on one side works well, or the curved piece of a broken clay pot or curved piece of driftwood will do the trick. Depending on what you're using as the basic building blocks of the whole thing you'll find something that will look nice at the top. Think outside the box and hunt through your junk drawer for inspiration.
13. Fill the bowl with water until it completely covers the top of the pump. Plug in the pump and enjoy your unique creation.

Chapter 8
Woodn't It Be Loverly

You're going down the street somewhere, and up ahead you see a "Garage Sale" sign. And in front of a home you see a lot of different things out for sale – furniture, lamps, tables of toys and books, maybe some jewellry and other knickknacks. So you remember what you read in that "Feminine Toolkit" book about looking at things a new way and decide to stop and check it out.

You see an old bedroom end table that is a nice shape, but the finish is all scuffed and the paint is peeling, maybe a knob is missing or even some of the wood is damaged. But overall it's in pretty good condition and you decide it would make a nice table for your telephone and the drawer would be perfect for your address book and a pencil and notepad for taking phone messages.

And just next to the end table you see an old rocking chair that has seen better days. The wooden seat is gouged and scratched, and the arms are worn. The seat pad is faded and stained, and covered in a hideous fabric that reminds you of a doctor's waiting room.

But the lady is willing to sell both to you for a total of $20. You think that with a few dollars of materials, that "Toolkit" book, and some imagination you can turn them into useful, maybe even eclectic, items. Maybe a gift for your niece who is moving into her own first apartment – she could use a few things to set up house.

So with these things in the trunk, you head to The Home Depot® or Rona® to pick up a few things you'll need to turn this trash into treasure.

Ordinary Wood items (not antiques or heirlooms)

If the items are ordinary wood (not an antique or anything), then you probably simply want to strip it down to the bare wood – take off the paint and any other finishes on it.

You can get "restorer" products that basically fix up the existing finish by filling in any scratches and resurfacing any areas where the finish is worn down. These work great on items with minimal problems.

But if they're that cheap particle board or plywood, then you certainly want to get to the bare surface before you do anything else.

To strip them down, you have a couple of options.

Take your time and do this part thoroughly and completely. Taking a shortcut here could result in a finished product that may not be exactly what you had in mind.

Sanding

If the piece is simply wood with a varnish or other clear finish on it, use a sander and gently sand all the finish off the wood. For nooks and crannies, you may need to use sandpaper to get into the small places.

The smaller the number on the sandpaper, the coarser it is and the rougher the final finish.

So start with 60-grit or 90-grit paper for the first sanding, then move to finer (higher numbers) grit for each subsequent sanding to get a smooth final finish. For the final sanding use fine steel wool to get a satin-like finish.

If the paint isn't too thick, you could try just using steel wool pads soaked with mineral spirits to work the paint off – this can be smelly, messy, sweaty work, but a great way to get some stress out of your system.

Chemical strippers

If it's painted, you can use the sanding technique, or you can use a chemical paint stripper. Most of these work very well – but do it outside, the fumes are unhealthy. Wear heavy rubber gloves, safety glasses and a dust mask.

Follow the directions on the label – usually you spread the stripper on the item with a brush or cloth, let it sit for a while to soak in, then remove it with a scraper.

Residue from stripping paint is both toxic and highly flammable. Dispose of it in a responsible manner. Put everything in a metal-covered container outside (like an old paint can or coffee can), as those materials can catch fire on their own if you're not careful.

Staining

If the item is real wood, and it's in good shape once you sand off all the paint and rough spots, you may just want to use a stain to bring out the grain of the wood, and when that's dry then apply a clear sealer coat.

Tip	When the dry sanding is finished, dampen the wood then let it dry. Sand with fine sandpaper. Do this two or three times until the grain doesn't rise any more. The reason: water causes the wood to expand and therefore the grain will rise, and means you need to sand again after staining. This means you take off some of the stain and have to do it again and again and ... This also applies if you want to paint the item (especially if you use a water-based paint).

1. The key is to put the stain on evenly and to keep your work area free of dust. So after sanding the item, use a tack cloth to get all the dust off.
2. Wet the wood with a little clear water using a wide, clean paintbrush. This helps the stain spread more evenly. Make sure that you have enough stain on hand for the job – if you run out and have to get more, it could be a different dye lot and the finish will be streaky or mis-matched.
3. Apply the stain (with) along the grain of the wood with a clean rag or paintbrush. Be generous – don't soak the wood but don't try to keep it thin. Brushes are better for carvings, molding and other irregularly shaped areas. Rags hold more stain and are easier to use on flat surfaces.
4. Wipe off excess stain with a paper towel.
5   Let dry, then apply another coat if there are patchy areas
6. When it's completely dry, apply a smooth light coat of varnish, shellac or wood polish to preserve the stain

Wood paint finishes

If the wood is in bad shape, it just doesn't look good, or if it's particle board or plywood, you probably want to paint the item.

Prime the entire piece with primer – if you're going to paint a dark colour get a primer intended to use under dark paint.

If the wood has a surface texture (like particle board sometimes does) you may want to apply two or three coats of primer (let it dry between coats). When it's dry, have a good time with your final finish. Use a faux paint finish, or glue on tissue paper to give a textured finish and then paint when the tissue is dry. Anything goes with one of these "junk yard finds".

A couple of years ago, a friend of mine mentioned he was moving into his own apartment and needed some small furniture pieces for his bedroom. The next weekend, I was driving around downtown Toronto and came upon a yard sale. It didn't look promising, but you never know.

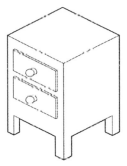

So I stopped and looked around, and I found a great little bedside table with drawers. It was painted glossy white (that was worn in some places) with a horrid bright glossy green trim paint. But the guy only wanted two dollars for it, so I grabbed it.

I didn't strip it down completely – it was just too many layers of paint on that thing. Under the white gloss was a sick yellow, then a pale blue under that, and then a brownish-grey under that. So I just sanded it down as well as I could.

Part of the back of the piece was broken loose, so I used wood glue (I used duct tape to hold the loose piece in place while the glue dried).

Then I primed the whole thing with two coats, then when that dried I painted the whole thing with a gloss black paint (it took 2 coats to get it smooth and even).

The drawers I faux-finished with a sponge dipped in black, tan, and gold craft paint to give it kind of a tortoise shell look.

I did the same paint technique along the top edge where the top sort of curves over.

I replaced the knobs with inexpensive brass-look ones left over from an old dresser of my mom's and it was just gorgeous.

Tip	Keep old knobs and other furniture hardware, even if the piece itself is no good. And pick up any you find at yard sales. They don't take up a lot of room, and you never know when they will come in handy.

Antiques or Heirlooms

If the item you want to refinish is a genuine antique, take it to a professional antique restorer.

Even something that you think is small and harmless like stripping and re-varnishing the piece could destroy the value and the beauty of the thing.

If it's not really an antique but is just old (maybe something from Grandma's basement or some dusty old thing you found somewhere), if you take your time and are careful you can end up with something really beautiful

If it's just a few nicks and scratches here and there, try one of the new "restorer" or "refinisher" products on the market – they're intended to fix up small imperfections in the finish without having to strip it down to the bare wood first.

Older furniture is usually made out of solid wood rather than particle board or plywood, and can be lovely when restored to their original beauty with some tender care and patience.

Like ordinary items, you will probably want to strip off any paint or varnish first. Use either the sanding or chemical method described earlier.

For solid wood items, I suggest that you use the staining technique discussed earlier. Good wood should be cherished and treated with respect to bring out the beautiful grain and colour, rather than covering it up with paint.

Chapter 9
Quick Fixits

There are a lot of things that at some time or another need fixing around your home. And if it needs to be fixed, guaranteed that there are tools and parts to fix it in one of the home improvement stores, plus advice on how to do it.

I've covered a few of the common fixits that are easy to do - every woman should be capable of handling these. I've done all these myself, often without any instructions. But if I bought a kit or something to replace that had instructions with it, I read them. Believe me, it's better than trying to sort through a little bag of parts that you don't recognize and trying to figure out where they all go.

I rate each fixit for you, based on:

Difficulty level   How hard I thought it was to do (on a scale of 1 to 10, with 10 being impossible for an ordinary mortal). This is assuming you have an average intelligence, can read directions in this book and on packaging, and have some common sense.

Time   How long I think it takes to do it right. It might take a professional less time that I state, and it might take you less or more time. Think of the time as a guide – if I say an hour, assume   it'll take probably about that, maybe more. Don't tackle that fixit if you've got 15 minutes one morning before you go to work.

Some cautions:

- If you're not sure you can do it, read the directions, check out the parts you'll need at a hardware store, ask the store clerk for advice, and research it for yourself. If you're still not sure, well that's what professional handymen are there for.
- Safety first. Wear safety glasses when working with wood, metal, or electrical. Work in well-ventilated areas, without clutter or trash in the way that could get into your project or cause a hazard.
- Keep small children and pets away from your work – they can be injured, or cause you to be injured.
- No alcohol or drugs before or while you're doing this – either can impair your motor skills and your judgment.

Replacing a screen

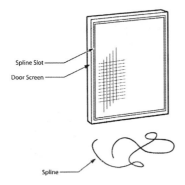

Spline Slot
Door Screen

Spline

Either a screen door or screen window gets a tear in it, or maybe it's just rusty or too dirty to clean.

Replacing the screen is very easy – in fact, you can often buy screen replacement kits in the home improvement or hardware stores. They usually have the screen fabric, the new spline, and a plastic tool to do the job easily.

Difficulty level: 2
Time: 30 minutes

What you need
- Screen replacement kit (large enough for the item you are doing)
- Flat head screwdriver
- Flat surface to work on that is large enough to lay your item down

How to do it
1. Measure - measure the length and the width of the frame you are re-screening (not sure if that's a real word, but I guess it is now). If you buy a rescreening kit, make sure the screen in the kit is several inches longer and wider than your frame.
2. Remove the old screen and frame - usually you can just lift up on the screen frame and pop the bottom out, then pull the top down and out as well. Once the frame is out, lay it down on a level surface so that the "spline" is up – that's a thin black rope that wedges into the frame to hold the screen fabric in place. Using a small flathead screwdriver or needle-nosed pliers, pull the old spline out and remove the old screen. Throw them both out.
3. Install the new screen - lay the new screen material over the frame so that it overlaps past the edge of the frame evenly all around. Make sure the "pattern" is square to the frame – if it's at an angle it won't stretch evenly and you'll get a wrinkled screen.

Starting in one corner, push the new spline into the groove so that it anchors the screen fabric into the frame (some kits come with a nifty little plastic tool to make this fairly easy). Keeping the screen fabric tight and straight, work down the frame pushing the spline into the groove as you go. Once you have done one side, do the opposite side pulling the screen fabric tight as you work. Then do the two remaining sides. Trim the excess screen fabric with a sharp knife or one of those small pens that hold sharp razor blades.

4. Install the frame - put the frame back in place. Push the top part up into the slot where it was originally – this should give enough room to pop the bottom back into place (you might have to hit it to pop it in).

Rewiring a lamp

Maybe you have a lamp you like that just won't work – I'll assume you've already replaced the bulbs and plugged the thing to test it in before you decided to rewire it.

So instead of buying a new lamp, rewire this one.

Note	If you feel you cannot safely tackle this project after reading the whole section, please have an electrician do it for you.

A lamp works because electricity runs through the 2-strand wire from the outlet, then the wire splits in the lamp base. When it's turned "on", the switch completes the circuit between the 2 wires and the electricity runs through the bulb – this is what causes the bulb to glow. When you turn it "off", the switch cuts off the electricity from one of the wires and it stops flowing into the bulb – so it stays dark.

Difficulty level: 4
Time: 1 hour

What you need
- The lamp you're fixing
- Lamp wire (long enough to run from the base where the bulb screws in, down the lamp, out the bottom, and to the outlet you're going to use
- Small flat-head screwdriver

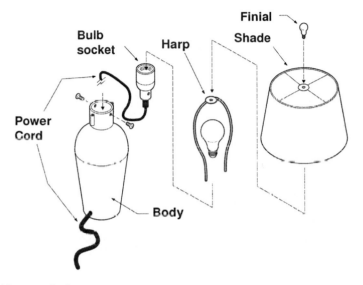

How to do it
If you're just replacing a lamp cord: unplug the lamp – I hope I didn't have to say it, but you never know what people might forget.

1. Disconnect the old cord from the lamp socket, and snip off the plug. Tie the new cord to the old one with a piece of string or some tape so you can use the old cord to pull the new cord through the lamp.

2. Cut off the old cord, toss it out. Tie a knot in the new cord, leaving about 3 inches to work with.

3. Strip about 1cm (1/2") of the insulation from the end of each wire.

4. Twist the strands tight with your fingers. Use needle-nose pliers to form hooks, and wrap them around the terminal screws. Tuck any loose strands in as you tighten the terminal screws.

5. Reassemble the socket and install the harp. Attach a new plug. You're ready to put in a bulb, attach the shade, and plug in your lamp.

Making your own lamp

That old vase with the hole in the bottom can be turned into a kitschy lamp if you're into that kind of thing. Basically anything with a hollow channel running through it can be turned into a lamp (it needs to be able to stand up on its own without danger of falling over – the bulb and lampshade add weight to the top, so the whole thing needs a good, weighted base to stand on. The taller the final lamp, the wider and the heavier the base needs to be to keep it stable.

Note	If you feel you cannot safely tackle this project after reading the whole section, please have an electrician do it for you.

Difficulty level: 6
Time: 1 hour

What you need
Look for a lamp wiring kit - it has everything you need. Otherwise, you'll need:

- Lamp bulb base – for indoor lamps, it's a brass-looking fixture that holds a bulb and connects the wires from the electric outlet to the lamp
- Light bulb appropriate for the fixture – standard-base bulbs are the common ones we're used to. Candelabra or chandelier-based bulbs have smaller bases, used in chandeliers and other similar light fixtures.
- Wire connectors – little "hats" with metal caps inside that are threaded to splice wires together – you screw the hats onto the wires you've twisted together, and the little caps inside grip the wire and hold it together. These also keep anything from touching these "live" connections
- Lamp wire (long enough to run from the base where the bulb screws in, down the lamp, out the bottom, and to the outlet you're going to use) – for most lamps, a #18 wire will do fine.
- Small flat-head screwdriver
- Wire strippers

How to do it

1. Make sure that whatever you're making into a lamp will stand up without tipping, and you can run the wire through it. You may need to attach some kind of base to the thing, like a square piece of wood and drilling a   hole through the bottom of the platform to run the wire through. Consider that a lamp is always top-heavy.

   If you're wiring the plug and lamp socket yourself, the attachment points are usually 2 screws and are different colours. The white or shiny point is the "neutral", and goes to the wide prong on the plug.

2. Attach the lamp socket base to your lamp by using a small threaded hollow pipe (this lets the lamp wire go down through the lamp). Attach this pipe to your lamp somehow – try gluing or screwing the pipe into the hole in your object. You can buy long threaded pipes in a lighting department – these pipes run the length of your lamp and tighten with small nuts at each end to keep it tight.

3. Make sure all the pieces are mounted before you run the wire through.

4. Fish the wire through the lamp – I use a straightened wire hanger with a small hook at one end that I tie the lamp cord to so I can pull it through. Almost like threading a drawstring in a waistband, only the lamp isn't flexible like a pair of pants (at least, pants should be flexible – if they aren't maybe it's time for laundry). If you don't want to do all this, you can get lamp bases that have the wire run outside the lamp, and you can glue the outside wire to the back of the lamp to keep it hidden.

5. Connect the plug to the wire, making sure the ridged wire is connected to the wide prong on the plug. Some plugs have a hole with a lever that lets you just poke the wire in the hole and connect it by closing the lever.

6. Attach the wires to the screw terminals – use wire strippers to remove about an inch of the wire's plastic insulation, then twist each wire to keep all the tiny wires it's actually made of together. Pull the two parts of the wire apart so there is enough space between the bare wires to let you connect each to their screw terminals.

7. Make a little hook in each wire, hook it around the terminal under the screwhead, then tighten – the screws tighten clockwise so your hook should have the open end to the right.

8. Reassemble the plug and the socket, making sure there's no excess wire sticking out. If the 2 wires touch, you'll short out the lamp, and could blow a fuse (well, I have a section on that too).

9. At the top of the bulb socket are two channels for the ends of the "harp". The harp is a metal arch that keeps the shade from resting on the bulb. Attach the harp, then attach the lampshade to the harp.

Installing a dimmer switch

Dimmer switches are basically dials or levers at the on-off switch for a lamp or light that reduces the amount of electricity flowing to the lamp, making it dimmer. You can have full brightness when you need it, then turn it down to a more relaxing or soothing light level when you don't need a lot of light.

Tips:	Don't use dimmers on fluorescent lighting. Don't use dimmers on a ceiling fan unless you get a dimmer made for a fan/light combo. Don't use dimmers on switches that control wall outlets, as you can damage something plugged in if that item needs full power to work (such as a vacuum cleaner).

There are different types of dimmer switches:

Single Pole switch: This switch affects a single light on a single electrical circuit (an example would be the switch on your bedroom wall that just controls the overhead light).

Three Way Switch: This switch works with another switch to control a light from two different places, e.g., when you can turn on the hall light from either end of the hallway. I don't recommend using a dimmer switch in this situation, but if you do, only install one - the other needs to be a toggle switch (the standard "on-off" switch).

Four Way Switches: These are not common, but can sometimes be found in very large rooms like banquet   halls or meeting rooms.   They are used in combination with a pair of 3 way switches to control lights from three or more locations.

Identifying the type of switch you have is as simple as counting the screws inside the switch. Single pole switches have 2 screw terminals, 3-way switches have 3 screw terminals, 4-ways have 4 screw terminals.

Make sure the dimmer you get is rated for the total wattage of whatever light fixture it's going to control. For example, if it's going to be for a chandelier that has five 100-watt bulbs, you want a dimmer that is rated for at least 500 watts. You'll find this information on the packaging of the switch.

Also, many dimmer switches don't come with the decorative cover, so get the cover at the same time to save a trip to the store.

Note	If you feel you cannot safely tackle this project after reading the whole section, please have an electrician do it for you.

Difficulty Level: 6
Time: 30 minutes

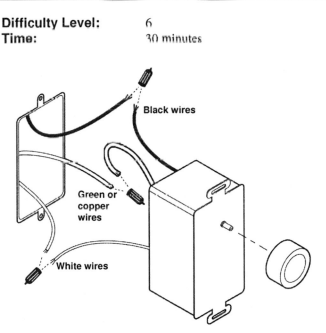

Black wires

Green or copper wires

White wires

What you need
- New dimmer switch
- Small flathead screwdriver
- Wire strippers

How to do it

Safety first - turn off the power. That doesn't just mean turn off the light at the switch. Nope, this is big-time electrical work.

At the fuse box, remove the fuse that serves that switch. If you have a circuit breaker box, flip the circuit breaker switch to off for that switch. If you don't know which fuse or circuit breaker is for that switch, either take out the fuses one at a time or flip the breakers on and off to see which one controls that switch. It's easier if you have someone to watch the light that this is for so they can tell you when the power is off. If you're on your own, you just have to check until you find the right one. Then label the fuse box or circuit box so you don't have to go through this again. Now, go back to the switch and flip it on to make sure there is no power in the switch.

If there is someone else in the house, use a strip of masking tape to cover the turned-off switch and write DO NOT TOUCH is big letters on the tape. Just in case your well-meaning friend decides to 'fix' your breaker, and lights you up instead. This can put a real strain on your friendship.

1. Remove the screws from the top and bottom of the old switch (a small flathead screwdriver is the best for this).
2. Take off the face plate and pull the entire switch box out of the wall – not too far, don't pull the wires out.
3. There are wires from the wall connected to wires in the switch box. Write down what colour wire from the wall is connected to what colour wire in the box.
4. Unscrew the plastic wire connector caps, un-twist the wires, and discard the old switch.
5. Connect one of the black wires – the "hot" wires that carry the power – from the wall to one from the dimmer switch. Do this by putting the bare wires next to each other and twisting them a little, then twist on a wire connector nut that came with the new switch.
6. Connect the white (neutral) wires the same way.

Note:	Some switches don't have the wires coloured, but they should be marked as to which is the "hot" wire - the one you connect to the black wire from the wall. That's why you wrote down which wires were connected to which in step 3 – just in case.

7. Connect the ground wires together (they're usually green). These are to protect your wiring in case the house is hit by lightning, or the circuit shorts out and the circuit breaker or fuse then cuts off the power to prevent a fire.

9. Make sure all the caps are tight and there is no bare wire showing.

10. If there is a lot of wire, it's okay – bend the wires over themselves (like a zig zag) and tuck them into the box inside the wall.

11. Push the new dimmer switch into place.

12. Adjust the switch until it's straight, then insert and tighten the two screws that hold it in place to the box in the wall.

13. Go back to your circuit breaker or fuse box and turn on the power to the switch.

14. If it's working, finish attaching the switch to the wall and put on the face plate.

Replacing a Fuse

 A fuse is a small item that stops the electrical wiring from shorting out the whole house if there is a short in a small appliance such as a toaster or hair dryer. They are about the size of a stack of 6 quarters, usually with a glass top and a base like the base of a light bulb. Fuses don't burn out the way a light bulb does, by just wearing out. The most common cause of a blown fuse is when you plug in and use an appliance (toaster, hair dryer, coffee maker) that has a defect or a short in it or if you use an appliance with a power rating higher than the fuse can take.

Household fuses are separate from the ones on your stove, so if your stove doesn't work check out the stove fusebox first (it's usually under the top decorative panel of the stove, but newer models could have them just about anywhere – check the owners manual). Be sure to turn off the stove circuit breaker or unplug the stove from the wall before playing around with the fuses.

You should have a few different fuses around in case one blows. They come in different ratings – little numbers visible through the glass and sometimes carved into the base as well. I'm not sure if the numbers refer to watts, amps, or volts - and I don't think it matters as long as you make sure the fuse rating stamped on the fuse matches the rating number on the fuse socket. I never did get electrical terminology, though I understand the basics of how electricity works.

You know a fuse has blown because:
1. There is no power in that outlet or light
2. The fuse for that circuit is burned out (its black or smoky inside)

Replace a blown fuse with one of the same number and size. But before you replace the fuse, unplug whatever appliance may have caused the fuse to blow in the first place. Either return the appliance (if it's new) or throw it out (if it's not new). Don't risk causing a fire or injury just to save a few dollars.

Some homes have breaker boxes, instead of fuse boxes. They don't use fuses, but just resetting the breaker may not solve the problem. If the breaker "tripped" due to faulty wiring or a short-circuit in an appliance, resetting the breaker could just cause it to trip again. If you know the reason for the breaker to trip (maybe you had a faulty hair dryer plugged in and you've unplugged it), then just throw the breaker switch back to the "on" position.

If you don't know the reason for the breaker to trip, call an electrician. No point in shorting out the whole house.

Note	If you feel you cannot safely tackle this project after reading the whole section, please have an electrician do it for you.

Difficulty level: 1-2
Time: 10 minutes

What you need
• A fuse of the right "power" to replace the blown fuse

How to do it

1. Identify which fuse has blown – visually check through the glass top of the fuse to see if it's burned out
2. Remove the burned-out fuse from the fuse box.
3. Screw a new fuse of the right power number into the receptacle you removed the old fuse from

Choosing a light bulb

Light bulbs are the simple little marvels of Edison's experiments over a century ago. Easy to buy and use. Right? Ah, but there are millions of different types of light bulbs out there (well, okay maybe not millions but there are a lot).

Selecting the type of light bulb is a little complicated. The type you use depends on your personal preference, plus what you're going to be using it for. So I thought I'd share what I have learned, to help you out when you need to light up your life.

Tip:	The number (wattage) on the bulb is a measure of how bright it gets – the larger the number, the brighter the light and the more energy used.

Incandescent

These are the most common bulbs you see everywhere. They're relatively inexpensive, but they're not very efficient - most of the energy going into the bulb ends up as heat, so they can burn out quickly. Which means you need several on hand, and that can get expensive over time.

Bulbs come in base sizes (the part that screws into the fixture):

Standard   For normal ordinary light fixtures and lamps.

Chandelier   Sort of says it in the name, these are bulbs with a small base (almost like Christmas lights) that fit into the smaller fixtures used in chandeliers.

Bulbs come in "temperatures", meaning the quality of the light

Cool white   These bulbs have a little blue in them, so the light itself is "cool". Use these for utility rooms such as kitchen bathroom, hallways.

Warm white   These bulbs have a little yellow in them, so the light itself is "warm". Use these for living areas such as living room, dining room, bedroom.

Bulbs come in "finishes":

Clear   The bulb itself is clear – the light is bright but it can cast shadows – you can see the filament which is not very attractive if the bulb is visible.

Frosted   The inside of the bulb has been coated so that the glass looks white – these have a nice soft light with few shadows in the room.

Bulbs come in "types":

Standard   The roundish shapes we're used to for most normal lamps

Flood   Large bulbs with an inner silvering that focuses the light out the top of the bulb – used when you want very directed lighting, e.g., to light a plant or picture. Often these are rather large and have a very flat top – sometimes the glass top has ridges and beveling (not sure why, maybe to scatter the light a bit so it's not so harsh. You can get smaller flood lights that are good for track lighting as it sends all the light out of the "hat" of the track light instead of some of the light staying in the fixture

Spot   These are like small flood bulbs, similar to a standard bulb but with a more flattened top

Tip	Flood lights and spot lights come with a "degrees" value that tells you how wide the spread of the light is. For example a 15-degree light is a fairly narrow cone of light, while a 30-degree light is wide enough to light a large painting or the keyboard of a piano. Of course, it also depends on how far away the light is from the thing being lit – the farther away, the dimmer the actual light, but the wider the area being lit.

Halogen

 These are very bright, very hot, very small bulbs. They can only be used in halogen lamps, and they look like clear glass beetles to me. Halogen bulbs last longer and are more efficient than incandescent bulbs. They are more expensive, but in the long run they can be a better deal since they do last a lot longer.

Fluorescent

These are the tube lights you see in most offices and other public areas. You will often also find them in homes in the bathroom or kitchen – the light is bright with few shadows.

You can also use fluorescent lighting under kitchen cabinets, home offices over the desk, or as strip lighting on either side of the bathroom mirror.

I've seen fluorescent fixtures that are actually very attractive in brass or black finishes, and they come in all styles and sizes – anywhere from 30cm (12") long to 150cm (5 feet) long.

Compact fluorescent bulbs can be used instead of normal incandescent bulbs – they are a low-cost, energy-efficient alternative to standard bulbs. They are 3-4 times more efficient than incandescent (meaning a compact fluorescent rated 9W is almost as bright as a 40W incandescent bulb).

So which bulb do you use?

Table/floor lamps   Standard incandescent or compact fluorescent bulbs. Most lamps have a label that indicates the maximum wattage for that lamp – don't go for more wattage than the fixture is rated for.
For living areas like the living room, dining room, bedroom – use a warm white bulb.
40W or 60W are usually bright enough for most living areas.

Torchiere lamps   These are the lamps that have a bowl on the top of a long rod, and the bulb sits in that bowl and shines upwards. For these, check the lamp rating – it may tell you what type of bulb you need. If it doesn't specify, then either a compact fluorescent or a spot light would be fine.

Desk lamps   Halogen lamps are brighter for desk or computer work, so you need halogen bulbs for these – watch the wattage of the bulb to make sure it matches the wattage for your lamp.
If going with an incandescent fixture, use a cool white bulb

Track lights   Check the fixture instructions – some have to be wired right into the wall, so you may want an electrician to do that for you. Others are "plug-in" types like an ordinary table lamp (this is what I have in my apartment). For non-halogen track lights, go with a flood bulb (check the fixture rating so you don't get a bulb with the wrong wattage).

Spot lights   I use this term for small lights you use to light up a painting, statue, or large plant. Others may call this accent lighting, or highlighting (no, not hair colour). Depending on the fixture you choose, you may need miniature fluorescent bulbs or small flood or spot lights

Recovering a chair or stool

Maybe those dining room chairs from your mom's basement are just dirty and can't be cleaned (I don't think you should ask Mom what the heck caused that stain, you might not really want to know the answer). Well, the chairs were free, so what do you want? Maybe you found a really cool chair at a garage sale (or better yet, at the curb the night before garbage day), but the fabric on the seat is just too revolting.

Or maybe you have a great chair but the vinyl seat has a nice hole in it from when you stood on the chair in your heels to hang a picture on the wall. Or maybe you're just tired of the fabric and you want a change. Whatever the reason, you have something upholstered that needs to be recovered.

I don't suggest you re-cover an entire sofa or recliner – just a little more work than I would tackle. But a dining room chair (seat only, or both the seat and the back) or bar stool, or even a small bedroom stool is easy to re-cover.

What you cover it with is up to you – fabric ends from a fabric store, sample swatches (as long as they're big enough), a blanket, bedsheet, or towel will also work.

Or make your own custom fabric by handpainting a piece of white fabric or canvas yourself – use fabric paints and follow the instructions on the paint to make sure the paint sets and doesn't come off with use.

Difficulty level: 4
Time: 30 minutes

What you need
- The fabric or other material you want to re-cover the item with
- Staple gun and staples
- Measuring tape
- Scissors (good heavy ones, not manicure scissors)
- Flat head screwdriver

- Fibre batting (sold in craft and fabric stores – be sure to get the flat sheet type, not the type used to stuff pillows)
- Foam padding (optional) at least 2.5cm (1") thick

How to do it

1. Remove the seat from the chair or stool frame – they're usually screwed in with a screw in each leg support.
2. Remove the existing covering – if it was stapled on, use an office staple remover or a small flathead screwdriver to pry up the staples. Be sure all staples, nails, or other metal fastenings are removed.
3. If the current padding is worn or old, remove as well.
4. If you are down to the bare wood or other hard material used to create the form of the seat, cover with foam padding, then a layer or 2 of the fibre padding. Trim both the foam and the fibre padding to the same shape as the hard form.
5. Cut your fabric so that it is at least 10cm (4") wider than your form in all directions.
6. Lay your final fabric layer face down on a flat surface, centre the rest of the assembled seat on the fabric, being careful to keep the foam and batting layers together.
7. Start in the centre of one side, pull the fabric up over the top of the form and staple in place.
8. Go to the opposite side of the seat, pull the fabric up over the top of the form, pull tight and staple in place.
9. Do the same on the 2 other sides.
10. Flip the form over to be sure the fabric is straight and looks good
11. Turn it back over right side down, and staple along each side so the fabric is tight and securely attached. One staple every inch should be enough – you don't need to completely "seal" the entire underside with staples.
12. In the corners, fold the fabric from one side over onto the adjacent side and staple in place – like wrapping a present at the corners.
13. Trim any excess fabric outside the staples.
14. Re-attach the chair seat to the leg frame, lining up the holes in the form with the holes in the leg frame. Use the same screws that you took out when you removed the form.

Repairing a wooden table or chair

If you have a chair or table that has a loose leg or edge, or if it's been broken, repairs can be fairly simple if the problem is not too severe.

The best solution: wood (carpenter's) glue. When it dries, wood glue is usually stronger than the wood itself.

Difficulty level: 3
Time: 20 minutes

What you need
- Wood glue
- Screwdriver to fit the screws on the piece
- Damp rag or cloth

How to do it
1. If necessary, take the item apart where it is screwed together. If it was put together with nails, be careful not to damage the wood when you take the nails out.
2. Spread an even, light coat of glue over the two broken surfaces and fit the wood together.
3. Use a rubber band or tight twine tightly around it to hold it together until the glue dries.
4. Wipe off any glue that leaks out while it's still wet – the glue will be relatively clear when it dries, but it does have a yellowish tint that may look a little trashy.
5. If you're gluing something that is flat, lay it down and cover with a cloth, then stack some books or other heavy objects on top to keep it together until the glue is dry.

If the screws are loose because the wood is cracked or worn, try screwing it together in a different place. If the wood inside the hole is in good condition but the hole has just enlarged over time, try using a larger-diameter screw to hold it together. If that doesn't work, or if the wood in the hole is chewed up, the simplest solution is to fill the hole completely with wood filler (it's like joint filler for the walls). Let it dry completely (at least 24 hours), then drill a pilot hole using a drill bit the diameter of the shaft of the screw you want to use. Fit the pieces in place and gently screw it together.

Replacing a toilet seat

So – your toilet seat has a nastily-placed crack in it (not nice, especially in the middle of the night when you're not really awake). Or maybe there is an interesting but disturbing stain that bleach and scrubbing just won't take out. Maybe you just want a new one, something more decorative than the institution-white that came with the apartment. Or maybe you're like my brother – you just want a nice soft, cushy seat. Whatever the reason, replacing a toilet seat is pretty easy.

Toilets come in basically 2 types – standard and low-flow. The type doesn't matter when you're replacing the seat, but the size and shape of the seat does matter.

Standard toilet seats are the ones you see hanging in the stores, and are the most common – they fit most normal toilets which are slightly oval (sort of, when you look down from the top).

Some toilets are more egg-shaped (sort of, when you look down from the top) and standard seats won't fit these.

Difficulty level: 2
Time: 20 minutes

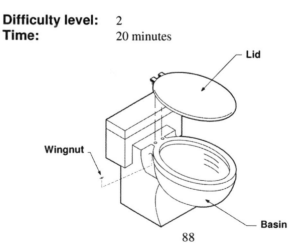

88

What you need

- New toilet seat and lid (you can find these almost anywhere – department stores, home improvement stores, hardware stores) – make sure the one you buy is the right size and shape for your toilet.
- Flathead screwdriver
- Adjustable wrench
- Lubricating oil (like WD-40® or other product)

How to do it

1. Close the old seat and lid so you can get at the bolts at the back that hold the seat onto the toilet bowl. If the bolts are covered with plastic caps, pop them off (use a screwdriver). Don't worry if they break – you aren't re-using them.
2. To remove the bolts, hold the nut underneath with the wrench while you loosen the bolt on top. If the bolt is really tight and you can't loosen it, use a squirt of WD-40® or lubricating oil onto the bolts and nuts, wait a few minutes for it to work on the rust or whatever is keeping the bolt stuck, then try again. If the bolt snaps or breaks, don't worry, you're not re-using these either.
3. Lift off the old seat and lid and throw them away (if they're in good condition, recycle them if possible). Clean the rim of the toilet bowl.
4. Align the holes on the new seat and lid with the holes that the old seat was bolted into
5. Put the new bolts (they should have come with the new toilet seat) into the holes in the seat and the bowl
6. Screw the nuts onto the bolts on the underside of the toilet. Tighten them with your fingers, and once you can't tighten them anymore, use your wrench to give them one more half-turn. Don't over-tighten the screws or you could crack the porcelain – then you have to replace the whole thing and for that I'd call a plumber.
7. Test the seat and lid a few times to make sure they move smoothly without any wobble. If it seems a little loose, tighten the bolts a little more (again, be careful).
8. Fit the plastic caps over the bolts, then celebrate – one more nasty item crossed off your "to-do" list.

Replacing a door knob

Maybe the door knob is tacky, maybe it's broken, maybe you just want something new. If the door knob you're replacing has a key lock/deadbolt, make sure you can complete the installation at one time – you don't want to stop installing a new lock and go to bed, leaving your home unsecured.

Tip	Before you buy a new doorknob assembly, measure the distance from the edge of the door to the centre of the doorknob – this tells you what size you need to buy. This is important, because the new doorknob needs to fit in the hole in the door exactly.

Difficulty Level: 6
Time: 1 hour

What you need
• Screwdriver (probably Phillips, but you might also need a flathead)
• Replacement lock/door knob set

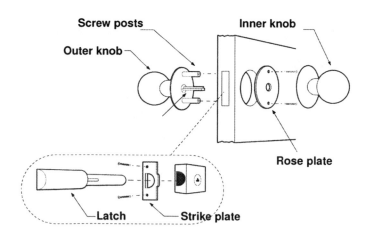

90

How to do it

Remove the old knob:

1. Remove trim (might be referred to as the "rose cover" – what a pretty name for a piece of metal). The trim is the decorative ring of metal that sits flush with the door to hide everything. There should be trim on both sides of the door (if not, then you definitely need to fix this). Unscrew the screws that hold this ring in place (they are usually in the side of the trim). Some models don't have screws - in this case, either turn the whole assembly counter-clockwise if the whole trim screws onto the backing plate, or pry the trim off with a small flathead screwdriver (be careful not to damage the wood of the door).

2. Remove the 2 screws holding the two sides of the knob in place

3. You should be able to pull the knob apart and out of the door completely – just grab both knobs and simply pull them apart and out of the door. Some knobs are held in place with a tiny screw in the side of the shaft. Be careful not to lose it – use a small flathead screwdriver to remove this screw.

4. Once they are out, you'll see two screws holding the deadlatch in place - remove both screws and pull the unit out.

5. If you want to replace the strike plate (the small flat metal plate that the bolt or latch slips into when the door is closed), remove the 2 screws holding it in place

Install the new knob:

Basically, this is doing what you did above only in reverse with the new knob. The packaging with the new knob may have directions and/or a diagram to help. If the new lock doesn't fit the existing hole, you may need to chisel some wood out, or use some sandpaper to smooth the wood.

1. Fit the new latch and deadbolt into place.

2. Insert the outer half into to the door hold, and align the connecting rods with the inside half,

3. Insert the long screws to secure it.

4. Install the new strike plate (if the one there right now doesn't match everything else)

5. Fit the trim and tighten the screws keeping the trim in place.

6. Test the mechanism with the door open, including the lock – if it doesn't work, you don't want to find out by closing the door and then not being able to open it.

Quick Fixits

Chapter 10
Brands, Stores, and Shopping

Brands and their comparisons

These are my **personal opinions** of the different brands of hand tools and power tools available in North America.

I make no claims to be an expert about these brands, how they are made, or who makes them. And I know people who will disagree with my opinions. Well, that's okay – people are entitled to their opinions.

So take these ratings any way you like – you can agree or not. Bottom line, when it comes to tools (or anything when you think about it), you have to buy from someone you trust.

Brand	Selection	Quality	Esthetics	Price
Craftsman® (Sears only)	★ ★ ★ ★	★ ★ ★ ★	★ ★ ★	★ ★ ★
Black & Decker®	★ ★ ★	★ ★	★ ★ ★	★ ★
DeWalt®	★ ★ ★ ★	★ ★ ★	★ ★	★ ★ ★
Skil®	★ ★ ★	★ ★	★ ★	★ ★ ★
Mastercraft® (Canadian Tire only)	★ ★ ★	★ ★	★ ★	★ ★ ★

The number of stars is my personal rating – the more stars the better (again, my personal opinion only).

Selection   The variety of products available – sizes, sets/collections, quality ranges

Quality   My opinion of the quality of the tools – how strong they are, how well-made, how well balanced

Esthetics   Okay, maybe not the most important factor when buying tools. But if the item is big and heavy and ugly, you may not be able to use it effectively. Most tools (especially power tools) are really designed for big burly guys on construction sites, not for the more dainty hands of a lady (and I'm a lady, regardless what my brother says).

Price   This is my thought on how affordable the brand is (in general) – the more stars, the better the value for your buck (not a rating of the actual prices, just my perceived value of the cost compared to the quality)

Remember, these are my **personal opinions only**.

Where I shop

You can buy national brand hand and power tools almost anywhere hardware, home improvement, retail, or do-it-yourself store. Some brands of tools are exclusive to a specific retailer (see the chart on the previous page).

The Home Depot® and Rona®

I like these stores for power tools, raw materials, paint, and bits and pieces for different projects. There are several reasons to shop here:
- the stores have all kinds of stuff you can use to decorate or to create projects
- the employees there are hired from the trades, they're not just high-school kids working part time. These people know what they're talking about, they have lots of great advice, and I always find the employees helpful and very friendly (I have asked some pretty stupid questions in my time, and while I'm sure they have a chuckle over it when I'm gone they have never made me feel dumb)
- the stores are very tidy and safe, and I find it easy to find things, even if I'm not sure exactly what the thing is called

And you can create quite a stir if you go on a Saturday afternoon in a nice skirt and nice heels – it'll turn a few heads, believe me. Why not make someone's day?

Home Hardware®

These are usually local stores, very convenient for all kinds of bits and pieces (you know, emergency duct tape and nails). The staff are usually very friendly and helpful, and they often have interesting items I don't see at other stores. They usually have good prices and good selections.

Sears®

In Canada and the U.S., Sears® carries national brand tools and they are the only place you can get the Craftsman® brand of tools. They carry all kinds of accessories and bits and pieces, but don't usually carry any of the raw materials for projects.

My power tool brand preference:	**Black&Decker®**
My hand tool brand preference:	**Craftsman®** (Sears Canada or US only)
My paint brand preference:	**Behr®**

Other places to check out:

Local hardware stores

Especially stores in smaller towns or old parts of the city – you know, the ones with creaky wooden floors and real old fixtures. You can find some interesting things if you're willing to get a little dusty. But I wouldn't go to these places for power tools or other technical things that really should have a warranty unless the store honours manufacturer warranties.

Garage and yard sales

It's amazing what some people throw out. A little paint, a little cleaning, maybe some new wire or handles, and you have a treasure. But don't look for technology here (stereo equipment, computers or printers, etc.) No warranty when you pay "Cousin Ed" five bucks for an inkjet printer. And no refunds if it doesn't work.

Be prepared to "negotiate" – items at a garage sale are intended to be very cheap. If it seems like a lot of money it probably is. Sometimes the seller adds in "emotional" or "sentimental" value to the price, but you're not paying for emotion or sentiment. You're buying something that, in a few days, will end up being thrown away. So even a couple of bucks from you is a good deal for both of you.

A friend of mine was looking for an office desk, and found a huge one for $50 bucks that would normally retail for about $350. It was in good shape (except for a couple of missing screws).

Bargain, discount, "dollar" and second-hand stores

You can find interesting beaded things, cheap foam brushes, plastic storage jars, and other stuff – just remember, you get what you pay for. Some things just shouldn't be cheap.

But these are great places to get clean-up rags (a.k.a. cheap face cloths) and nailpolish remover to take spray paint off your hands or the floor. Also great places for small plastic storage containers to hold bits and pieces, for duct tape and glue, etc. Look around and you'll be surprised what you might find.

Other shopping

I thought I'd toss these in for you. I don't just shop in hardware or home improvement stores - yes, I do other things besides fix stuff around the house. I shop for household cleaning, personal care, clothes, and other things just like you. And these stores are just my personal preferences, not a judgement of the value of other stores you may prefer.

Cosmetics, Skin Care, and Personal Care

I prefer **Quixtar.com**® for my personal care items such as cosmetics, skin care, hair care, etc. I like the convenience of shopping on the Internet, and having it delivered to my house usually within 3 business days (most online shopping takes up to 2 weeks).

These are the brands I buy – it saves me a lot of time shopping since I don't have to check out drug stores and department stores all the time:

Cosmetics   **Artistry**®

Skin Care   **Artistry**®

Hair Care   **Satinique**® (shampoo, conditioner, leave-in conditioner, hair styling). Since I colour my hair (sorry to disappoint anyone, but no, I'm not a natural blond) so I use their new Capture Colour® hair care products.

If you want to shop for cosmetics and personal care items from Quixtar, try this website: **www.lmentze.qbeautyzone.com.** It's secure and simple to use.

Jewellry

Well, I have to admit I make most of my own costume jewellry – I find beads in the craft section of **Wal-Mart**, or in cheap bracelets or necklaces at discount stores. Then I take them apart and string my own creations. I get something inexpensive and unique.

Laundry and household cleaning

Quixtar.com® again. For laundry, I buy the tablet form of the **SA8** detergent – it comes in 2 boxes totaling 96 tablets. I do one or two loads of laundry a week; at one tablet per load of laundry, this one purchase lasts almost two years before I have to buy more. One less thing to have to carry home from the grocery store, and a lot less garbage into landfill. For cleaning, I like the **L.O.C.** line of products – they're concentrated so they go a long way and I have to buy them less often than ordinary grocery-store items.

Beads and other small craft items

Wal-Mart® has a good-sized craft section, with a lot of nice glass and wooden beads and jewellry findings.
Michael's® is a great all-around craft store with a wide variety of all kinds of craft items and home décor items.

Car Care

In Canada, **Canadian Tire Co.** ® has a great automotive section and knowledgeable sales staff. Not just parts for you to do your own work, but they provide most automotive repairs and maintenance services.

Vitamins and other Nutritional Supplements

Quixtar.com® once again. It's the only place to get Nutrilite® vitamins and supplements. I used to buy whatever was on sale in the drug store, but I did some research and realized that most of the supplements I was taking were just going straight through my system. Nutrilite® is certified organic, and the research and development they do is world-class.

My health is important to me. My mom and grandmother both ended up with health problems once they reached their 60's, and I plan to stay healthy and active long past that age. By taking the right supplements now, I can keep my system in top condition (like regular car maintenance). I don't want my life controlled by doctors and prescription drugs with side-effects worse than the condition they're treating.

Brand, Stores, and Shopping

A Final Word (or 2)

So how are things going? Have you learned something you can use from all this? Did you enjoy the book? I certainly enjoyed writing it – all the stories and tips are true (only the names have been changed to protect the innocent).

But there is one thing I hope everyone that reads this book learns - **you can do it if you want to.**
So many things in life can be looked at more than one way. But so often we are taught "this is the way" and any other way to look at things is weird, or not normal, or "just not right".

Copper tubing is just for plumbing fixtures, right?
Nope – copper tubes can be wind chimes or decorative sculptures, or something I haven't even thought of.

Shoes only come in the colours the manufacturer makes them - right?
Nope – they can be any colour; all you have to do is paint them.

Broken dishes should be thrown away – right?
Nope – they can be decorative "stones" in a clear vase, the base of a do-it-yourself mosaic table or stepping stones, or glued on a plant pot.

Walls should be a plain paint colour – right?
Nope – paint is like clothing accessories. Go with what you like, not what "they" say is normal.

Some things girls are just not good at – right?
Nope – women can do anything they want, it's just a matter of learning how and then doing it.

So tell me what you've learned. What projects you decided to tackle, and how you made out. Did you try something that isn't even in this book? I'd love to know all about it. Email me at **ToolKit@rogers.com** Maybe your story will be in my next book! And check out my website at **www.LindaUnbridaled.com** for tips and ideas on living the single life.

A Final Word (or 2)

Time to Go Shopping

Use this list of my recommended tools to help you "inventory" what you already have and what you still may need to buy.

Hand Tools

Item	Size	Have	Need
Hammers			
Claw hammer	240-375 gm (8-12 oz) 28-30 cm (11-12")		
Screwdrivers			
Flat head	28-30 cm (11-12")		
Flat head	7-9 cm (4-6")		
Phillips	Size 2 (red handle)		
Robertson	Size 1 (green handle)		
Robertson	Size 2 (red handle)		
Mini set			
Pliers			
Slip Joint	20 cm (8")		
Needle-nose	14 cm (6")		
Wirecutter			
Wrenches			
Adjustable	25 cm (10")		
Locking	13-14 cm (5-6")		
Torque set			
Saws			
Hand saw	30 cm (12")		
Hacksaw	20 cm (8"), plus blades		
Pipecutter	32-.64cm (1/8" to 1/4") outside diameter		
Pipecutter	.64-5cm (1/4" to 2") outside diameter		

Other Tools

Item	Size	Have	Need
Staple Gun	Plus staples		
Scraper	2.5 cm (1")		
Scraper	9 cm (4")		
Utility knife	Plus blades		

Power Tools

Item	Comments	Have	Need
Cordless Drill	Reversible, variable speed		
Drill Bits	Mixed set incl. screwdriver bits		
Small sander	Plus replacement sandpaper		
Glue Gun	Plus glue sticks to fit		
Bits and Pieces			
Nuts and bolts			
Screws, nails			
Washers			
Hooks			
Duct Tape			
Epoxy Glue			
Heavy-duty glue			
Wood glue			
Twine			
Picture hanging	Wire, hooks		
Lamp parts			
Extension cords	Heavy-duty, grounded		
Tack cloth			
Safety glasses			
Dust masks			

Paint and Wallpaper

Item	Comments	Have	Need
Latex paint	Satin finish		
Craft brushes	3 or 4 small ones		
Paint brush	5-8 cm (2-3")		
Roller handle			
Roller covers			
Roller tray			
Tray liner			
Broom handle	To extend roller handle		
Wallpaper tray			
Kitchen sponges			
Sea sponge			
Wallpaper smoother			
Seam roller			
Painters tape			

Bits and Pieces

Item	Comments	Have	Need
Duct Tape			
Asst. screws			
Asst. bolts			
Asst. nails			
Glue			
Twine			
Sandpaper			
Dust Masks			
Safety Glasses			
Lubricant			
Measuring tape			

Other Projects

Item	Comments	Have	Need
Lamps			
Lamp wire			
Lamp parts			
Water Fountain			
Pump			
Container			
Decorations			
Replacing a screen			
Screening	A kit usually has everything you need		
Others			
Doorknob			
Fuses			
Toilet seat			
Lightbulbs			
Dimmer switch			

Index

Index

About the Author

Linda was born in 1956 in Vancouver, B.C., Canada of immigrant German parents, with one younger brother joining the family when she was three years old.

Her first experience with home repairs was when she was ten years old and her father decided to install a small second bathroom in the basement of their three-bedroom home – a project that ended up taking almost 6 months to complete and never did work all that well.

Linda had a number of different jobs in high school and college, her first permanent job coming in 1976 when she started working for Simpsons-Sears Canada (now known as Sears Canada Inc.) as a salesclerk in the shoe department. Ten years later she was transferred to the corporate head office in Toronto Ontario. Twenty years as a corporate training consultant has given Linda the opportunity and education to teach others on all manner of topics, and that is where she honed her writing and public speaking skills.

Linda learned about home repairs and tools the simple way – by trial and error, by doing it wrong and learning from her mistakes.

She watches all the home improvement shows, "For all the creative ideas, for making neat things on a shoestring budget."

She currently lives in Toronto, Ontario with her pet parrot Sagan.

Printed in the United States
84855LV00001B/130-135/A